DATE DUE

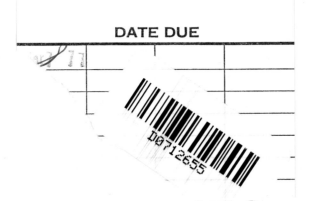

D0712655

China
&
the U.S.
1955-63

China
&
the U.S.
1955-63

Edited by Kwan Ha Yim
Chairman, Department of Political Science
Manhattanville College (Purchase, N.Y.)

FACTS ON FILE, INC.   NEW YORK, N.Y.

China
&
the U.S.
1955-63

Library of Congress Catalog Card No. 72-80832
ISBN 0-87196-206-3

9 8 7 6 5 4 3 2
PRINTED IN
THE UNITED STATES OF AMERICA

CONTENTS

Page

i

THE U.S. AND CHINA HAVE DEVELOPED an extraordinary pattern of bilateral relations since the Chinese Communists expelled the Nationalist government from mainland China in 1949. In the absence of normal diplomatic contacts, U.S.-Chinese relations were conducted largely through the medium of the press and through another modern device: sending signals by guns. These practices supplemented the ancient diplomacy by hostage. Communist China—more formally the People's Republic of China—held American prisoners from the Korean War and used them to exact concessions from the U.S.

The basic issues in U.S.-Chinese relations crystalized in an early stage of the confrontation. Peking wanted the U.S. out of Taiwan (Formosa) and the Taiwan Straits. The U.S. was determined to prevent the forcible seizure by Communist China of Taiwan—seat of the anti-Communist Nationalist régime known as the Republic of China—and of the islands along the Chinese coast that were under Nationalist control. For Communist China, the extension of its rule to the Nationalist-held islands was a matter of completing its revolution and of attaining national unity. For the U.S., the withdrawal of its support from the Nationalist Chinese on Taiwan and the off-shore islands initially meant the surrender of the islands and their inhabitants not just to another Chinese government but to the monolithic Communist world.

The Chinese Nationalist-Communist rivalry antedated the Cold War by 2 decades. Both the Communist and Nationalist movements in China had developed as a protest against the intrusion by Western powers on Chinese sovereignty and the warlord-controlled government of the 1920s. At first they were united in the Kuomintang (Nationalist Party) under

1

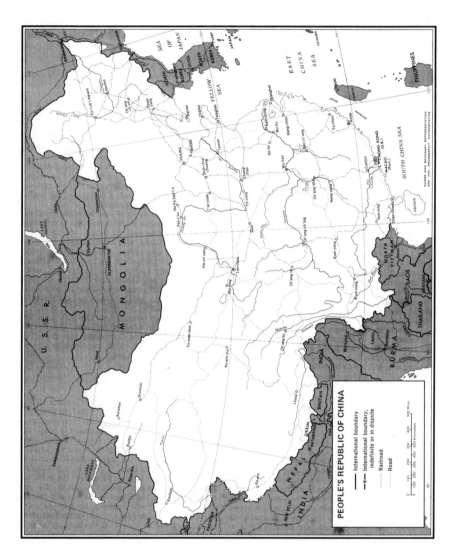

PEOPLE'S REPUBLIC OF CHINA

International boundary
International boundary, indefinite or in dispute
Railroad
Road

Dr. Sun Yat-sen, but soon they parted company because of ideological differences. During the Sino-Japanese War of 1937–45, the 2 groups joined in an uneasy, suspicion-filled alliance, and the U.S. fought on the side of the Chinese against Japan. But as soon as the war against Japan was over, civil war broke out again, resulting in the defeat and withdrawal of the Nationalists late in 1949 to their island bastion on Taiwan. A U.S. effort in 1945–7 to mediate and thus to forestall Communist-Nationalist conflict had proven wholly ineffective.

The basic themes of the U.S.-Communist Chinese disputes, repeated for more than 2 decades by both sides, would have made a tedious tale had it not been for rapidly changing events and developments on the world scene that provided a setting for seemingly endless variations of those themes. The Taiwan issue became a Cold War issue, and the changing nature of the Cold War gave the Taiwan issue a different complexion and meaning.

The narrative in this volume begins with an account of the first Taiwan (Formosa) crisis, the crisis of 1955, which led to the adoption by the U.S. Congress of the so-called "Formosa Resolution"; it ends with the sudden close of the Kennedy Administration in 1963. The material, compiled by FACTS ON FILE, is based largely on contemporary press reports; it is, therefore, not intended as a definitive history, which would require additional research and the use of yet unavailable archival materials. Because of the peculiar circumstances, much of what occurred between the U.S. and Communist China took place in public. This volume, therefore, gains a usefulness surpassing its modest claims. As in all FACTS ON FILE books, great pains were taken to present all material, however controversial, without bias.

TAIWAN STRAITS CRISIS OF 1955

Efforts to Free U.S. Captives in China

In 1955, more than 5 years after the establishment by the Communists of the People's Republic of China, the U.S. government and the bulk of its citizenry were generally hostile to the régime in Peking. Many Americans were angered over the incarceration by Communist China of some 50 Americans, including soldiers who had been taken prisoners of war during the Korean conflict (1950–3). 11 of these prisoners, members of the U.S. Air Force, had been jailed in Nov. 1954 on charges of spying.

The Eisenhower Administration brought the case before the UN General Assembly. The General Assembly adopted a resolution calling on Secy. Gen. Dag Hammarskjöld to use his good office in securing the release of the imprisoned fliers.

Hammarskjöld made a trip to Peking in Jan. 1955, stopping en route in London, Paris and New Delhi to confer with British, French and Indian leaders. Indian Prime Min. Jawaharlal Nehru, opposed to Hammarskjöld's mission because Communist China had taken no part in the UN debate on the case of the captured Americans, waited a full day— until Jan. 3—to meet with the Secretary General. He was said to have rejected Hammarskjöld's request that a senior Indian diplomat be assigned to help conduct the talks in Peking. The Indian government assigned low-ranking Foreign Office officials to greet Hammarskjöld when he landed in New Delhi Jan. 2 and see him off the next day.

Hammarskjöld arrived in Peking Jan. 5. He met informally and dined with Communist Chinese Premier-Foreign Min. Chou En-lai prior to formal talks beginning Jan. 6. Talks were held by Chou and Hammarskjöld Jan. 6, 7, 8 and 10 on the fate of the 11 American Korean War fliers. Chou and Hammarskjöld Jan. 10 then issued a com-

5

muniqué saying only that "these talks have been useful, and we hope to be able to continue the contact established in these meetings." The conversations were held in private, and Hammarskjöld declined to reveal their content until he had returned to New York and reported to the UN delegations concerned.

The UN Secretariat announced Jan. 11 that Hammarskjöld would confer with U.S. Amb.-to-UN Henry Cabot Lodge as soon as he arrived back in New York. The statement asserted that the Secretary General had not failed in his mission. On the contrary, it said, Hammarskjöld "has made progress toward the goal set for him by the General Assembly. The talks in Peking...established a basis upon which further progress can be made."

Hammarskjöld returned to New York Jan. 13. He described his trip as "a first stage" in the effort to secure the release of the 11 American fliers and other UN Command personnel still detained in mainland China. "I feel that my talks with Mr. Chou En-lai were definitely useful for this purpose," he said. "We hope to be able to continue our contact. The door that has been opened can be kept open, given restraints on both sides."

Hammarskjöld conferred with U.S. Amb. Lodge Jan. 13. At a press conference Jan. 14, Hammarskjöld emphasized in connection with the prisoners that "no deals of any kind" were made or suggested by either side during his Peking talks. Speaking generally, Hammarskjöld said that it would be "useful" if Communist China were a member of the UN. He also linked prospects of the fliers' release with a lessening of tensions between Communist China and the U.S.

U.S. Reaction to Hammarskjöld's Trip

U.S. State Secy. John Foster Dulles said in an address at a YWCA centennial luncheon in New York Jan. 11, 1955 that Americans "eagerly await" Hammarskjöld's report on his return from China and meantime were making a "contribution to the peaceful settlement of these issues by heeding the biblical instruction to be 'slow to anger.'" Other voices were less restrained.

Adm. Arthur W. Radford, U.S. Joint Chiefs of Staff chairman, said in Washington Jan. 11 that an Allied blockade of mainland China "would have a great deal of effect on the Red Chinese" and, as a last resort to force release of the 11 fliers, "would be the best way to tackle such a problem." (A Joint Chiefs spokesman said later that Radford, in answering a reporter's question about the effectiveness of a blockade, did not intend to advocate such a measure and still believed the decision should be Pres. Dwight D. Eisenhower's.)

Sen. H. Alexander Smith (R., N. J.) said Jan. 11 that he would favor a blockade as a last-ditch action if it were imposed by the UN.

U.S. Air Force headquarters in Washington reported Jan. 12 that photos from mainland China had displayed these items of "evidence" that captured American airmen were spies: (1) a portable radio, standard equipment on U.S. planes flying in combat or over dangerous territory; (2) a rescue device—standard with military and civil aviation in many countries—represented by Communist China as an invention for scooping a U.S. agent off the ground in China.

The White House joined Dulles in urging Americans to be patient. In a statement issued Jan. 14, Pres. Eisenhower expressed "disappointment" at the continued imprisonment of the 11 fliers. But he urged the people not to "fall into a Communist trap" by calling for "reprisal or retaliation."

U.S. Senate minority leader William F. Knowland (R., Calif.) said Jan. 17 that Hammarskjöld's trip "was a failure by any fair standard that Americans can use." Knowland, who had advocated a blockade of mainland China to force the release of the fliers, said in an address before the Newspaper Advertising Executives Association in convention in

Chicago that Congress would carefully scrutinize any attempt to appease Communist China.

Dulles said Jan. 18 that it was too early to pass final judgment on Hammarskjöld's mission. He asserted that the U.S. would have to deal with the matter itself if the UN failed to obtain freedom for the fliers. He fixed no exact time-limit for concluding that the UN had failed. Hammarskjöld went to Washington Jan. 19 at Dulles' request to give the State Secretary an account of the Peking talks.

Fighting in Taiwan Straits

Meanwhile, Chinese Communist and Nationalist forces clashed again in the Taiwan Straits. 4 days after Nationalist bombers had attacked the mainland seaport town of Haimen Jan. 14, 1955, Communist Chinese troops borne on 100 motorized junks Jan. 18 captured the 3-square-mile Nationalist-held island of Yikiang (Yikiangshan), 8 miles from the Tachen Islands (which had themselves been heavily bombed Nov. 1-4, 1954 by Communist planes). The invaders were supported by naval and artillery fire from neighboring Communist-held islands and a bombing assault from 60 warplanes. Nationalist reports said that remnants of a guerrilla force of 2,000 men on the island continued to offer strong resistance through Jan. 19. More than 200 Communist planes bombed the Tachens Jan. 19 in the heaviest assault of the coastal war. The Communists also landed reinforcements Jan. 19 on Yikiang, near the Tachens, and shelled nearby Pi (Pishan) Island heavily. The Nationalist air force struck back by bombing Communist shipping along a 300-mile coastal stretch of the Chinese mainland.

The Nationalist Chinese Defense Ministry announced Jan. 21 that the last of 720 guerrilla defenders on Yikiang Island had succumbed to Communist Chinese invaders the previous night after killing 1,500 of the attackers. The ministry reported heavy Nationalist air attacks Jan. 20 in the Foochow area of Fukien Province. It said that at least 44 Communist craft, including 9 gunboats, had been sunk.

Vice Adm. Alfred M. Pride, commander of the U.S. 7th Fleet, arrived in Taipei from Hong Kong Jan. 23 and went into immediate conference with American and Nationalist Chinese officials, including Generalissimo Chiang Kai-shek. Pride reportedly went to Taiwan to make plans for 7th Fleet participation in an evacuation of Nationalist forces from the Tachens, where Communists had already achieved air and naval superiority. The Nationalist government reportedly agreed "in principle" to such an evacuation Jan. 26, but a Nationalist official said that final consent would depend on whether or not the evacuation was related to a UN cease-fire move, which the Chiang Kai-shek government strongly opposed. A small group of civilian evacuées from the Tachens arrived on Taiwan Jan. 25 by ship without a U.S. escort.

Neither Yikiang nor the Tachens was essential to the defense of Taiwan and the Pescadores, according to press conference statements by U.S. State Secy. Dulles Jan. 18 and Pres. Eisenhower Jan. 19. Dulles indicated that the U.S. 7th Fleet, which was operating in Taiwan Strait, would not become involved in the Tachen-area fighting. The President said that he did not even know whether the Nationalists planned a strong defense of the Tachens. Eisenhower said that he would like to see the UN "exercise its good offices" to bring about a cease-fire in Taiwan Strait, but he observed that both the Nationalist and Communist Chinese might insist that their warfare was an internal dispute not within the UN's jurisdiction.

Communist Chinese Premier-Foreign Min. Chou En-lai Jan. 24 reasserted his government's intention to conquer Taiwan. (He had first advocated that course Aug. 11, 1954 and had warned "foreign aggressors" who might intervene of "grave consequences.") Chou rejected any idea of a cease-fire in the Taiwan area and accused the U.S. of "using war threats brandishing atomic weapons to force the Chinese people into tolerating" the "occupation" of Taiwan. Chou's statement, broadcast by Peking radio, said that American forces must leave Taiwan and stop "interfering in Chinese internal affairs." Chou accused the U.S. of using the Communist conquest of Yikiang Island as an excuse for increasing "its military operations to make war provocations." He cited part of Article 2, Paragraph 7 in the UN Charter, which prohibits UN intervention in the domestic affairs of any state, in his argument that the UN had no right to intervene in the threatened conquest of Taiwan.

U.S. to Defend Taiwan

The U.S. and the Nationalist government on Taiwan had signed a mutual defense pact Dec. 2, 1954. The treaty guaranteed Taiwan and the Pescadores against attack from the mainland. In a letter to State Secy. Dulles Dec. 10, Nationalist Chinese Foreign Min. George K. C. Yeh stated that Nationalist China would not attack the mainland without U.S. approval. The treaty was approved 360-0 by the Nationalist Chinese Legislative Yuan in Taipei Jan. 14, 1955, with no abstentions.

Pres. Eisenhower Jan. 6 sent a message to the U.S. Senate urging an "early" action. The Democratic members of the Senate Foreign Relations Committee had received a private memo from the Democratic National Committee challenging the wisdom of the U.S.-Nationalist defense pact.

The Americans for Democratic Action (ADA) Jan. 16 labeled the mutual defense treaty with Nationalist China a potential "political boobytrap." The ADA argued that through ratification of the treaty, the U.S. would recognize the Taiwan and Pescadores as territories of China, "giving substance to the Communist claim...that invasion... would be merely an extension of the civil war rather than international aggression." 3 members of the Senate Foreign Relations Committee (Sens. Hubert H. Humphrey, D., Minn.; William F. Knowland, R., Calif.; and Mike Mansfield, D., Mont.), which was considering the pact, said Jan. 16 that they would support it despite some reservations.

The U.S. Senate Feb. 9 approved the ratification of the treaty by 64–6 vote, and Pres. Eisenhower ratified it Feb. 11. The treaty took effect Mar. 3, 1955 with the exchange of ratification instruments in Taipei. *The text of the treaty:*

The parties to this treaty,

Reaffirming their faith in the purposes and principles of the Charter of the United Nations and their desire to live in peace with all peoples and all governments, and desiring to strengthen the fabric of peace in the West Pacific area,*

Recalling with mutual pride the relationship which brought their 2 peoples together in a common bond of sympathy and mutual ideals to fight side by side against imperialist aggression during the last war,

Desiring to declare publicly and formally their sense of unity and their common determination to defend themselves against external armed attack, so that no potential aggressor could be under the illusion that either of them stands alone in the West Pacific area, and

Desiring further to strengthen their present efforts for collective defense for that preservation of peace and security pending the development of a more comprehensive system of regional security in the West Pacific area,

Have agreed as follows:

Article I—The parties undertake, as set forth in the Charter of the United Nations, to settle any international dispute in which they may be involved by peaceful means in such a manner that international peace, security and justice are not endangered and to refrain in their international relations from the threat or use of force in any manner inconsistent with the purposes of the United Nations.

Article II—In order more effectively to achieve the objective of this treaty, the parties separately and jointly by self-help and mutual aid will maintain and develop their individual and collective capacity to resist armed attack and communist subversive activities directed from without against their territorial integrity and political stability.

Article III—The parties undertake to strengthen their free institutions and to cooperate with each other in the development of economic progress and social well-being and to further their individual and collective efforts towards these ends.

---

*The term "West Pacific area" was understood to mean principally Japan, the Philippines and Indonesia.

Article IV—The parties, through their foreign ministers or their deputies, will consult together from time to time regarding the implementation of this treaty.

Article V—Each party recognizes that an armed attack in the West Pacific area directed against the territories of either of the parties would be dangerous to its own peace and safety and declares that it would act to meet the common danger in accordance with its constitutional processes. Any such armed attack and all measures taken as a result thereof shall be immediately reported to the Security Council of the United Nations. Such measures shall be terminated when the Security Council has taken the measures necessary to restore and maintain international peace and security.

Article VI—For the purposes of *Articles II* and *V*, the terms "territorial" and "territories" shall mean in respect of the Republic of China, Taiwan and the Pescadores; and in respect of the United States of America, the island territories in the West Pacific under its jurisdiction. The provisions of *Articles II* and *V* will be applicable to such other territories as may be determined by mutual agreement.

Article VII—The government of the Republic of China grants, and the government of the United States of America accepts, the right to dispose such United States land, air and sea forces in and about Taiwan and the Pescadores as may be required for their defense, as determined by mutual agreement.

Article VIII—This treaty does not affect and shall not be interpreted as affecting in any way the rights and obligations of the parties under the Charter of the United Nations or the responsibility of the United Nations for the maintenance of international peace and security.

Article IX—This treaty shall be ratified by the United States of America and the Republic of China in accordance with their respective constitutional processes and will come into force when instruments of ratification thereof have been exchanged by them at Taipei.

Article X—This treaty shall remain in force indefinitely. Either party may terminate it one year after notice has been given to the other party.

Shortly after the military clash in the Taiwan Straits, Pres. Eisenhower Jan. 24 had sent a special message to Congress requesting emergency authorization to use U.S. armed forces to protect Taiwan and the Pescadores Islands. In his message, the President said:

● The U.S. and all free nations had a common interest that Taiwan and the Pescadores "should remain in friendly hands." Under these circumstances, the U.S. 7th Fleet had defended Taiwan and the Pescadores from Communist attack since 1950 and would continue to do so.

● Earlier Communist air, artillery and amphibious attacks on Quemoy and the Tachens, in addition to Peking's avowed intention to "liberate" Taiwan, had made it necessary for the U.S. to be ready to (1) assist in the redeployment and consolidation of Nationalist forces (an indirect reference to a possible evacuation of the Tachens) and (2) "take appropriate military action" against Communist forces massed on near-by islands or on the mainland for an invasion of Taiwan.

● The U.S. Administration believed that the situation was appropriate for Taiwan Strait cease-fire efforts by the UN. The current critical situation, however, required the U.S. to take steps for peace without awaiting UN action.

● The emergency powers sought by the President were no substitute for the mutual defense treaty already signed with Nationalist China. It had become more important than ever that this pact be approved and put into force.

After the reading of the President's message Jan. 24, identical resolutions embodying his requests were introduced by House Foreign Affairs Committee Chairman James P. Richards (D., S.C.) and Senate Foreign Relations Chairman Walter F. George (D., Ga.). This "Formosa Resolution" gave Eisenhower unlimited authority to use U.S. armed forces for the security of Taiwan and the Pescadores. They said that the authority would expire "when the President shall determine that the peace and security of the area is reasonably assured." (It was commonly understood that the term "armed forces" in the resolutions referred only to naval and air power, since the Administration believed Nationalist Chinese ground forces were sufficient.)

The text of the "Formosa Resolution":

A joint resolution authorizing the President to employ the armed forces of the United States for protecting the security of Formosa, the Pescadores and related positions and territories of that area

Whereas the primary purpose of the United States, in its relations with all other nations, is to develop and sustain a just and enduring peace for all; and

Whereas certain territories in the West Pacific under the jurisdiction of the Republic of China are now under armed attack, and threats and declarations have been and are being made by the Chinese Communists that such armed attack is in aid of and in preparation for armed attack on Formosa and the Pescadores,

Whereas such armed attack if continued would gravely endanger the peace and security of the West Pacific area and particularly of Formosa and the Pescadores; and

Whereas the secure possession by friendly governments of the Western Pacific Island chain, of which Formosa is a part, is essential to the vital interests of the United States and all friendly nations in or bordering upon the Pacific Ocean; and

Whereas the President of the United States on January 6, 1955, submitted to the Senate for its advice and consent to ratification a Mutual Defense Treaty between the United States of America and the Republic of China, which recognizes that an armed attack in the West Pacific area directed against territories, therein described, in the region of Formosa and the Pescadores, would be dangerous to the peace and safety of the parties to the treaty: Therefore be it

Resolved by the Senate and House of Representatives of the United States of America in Congress assembled, That the President of the United States be and he hereby is authorized to employ the Armed Forces of the United States as he deems necessary for the specific purpose of securing and protecting Formosa and the Pescadores against armed attack, this authority to include the securing and protection of such related positions and territories of that area now in friendly hands and the taking of such other measures as he judges to be required or appropriate in assuring the defense of Formosa and the Pescadores.

The resolution shall expire when the President shall determine that the peace and security of the area is reasonably assured by international conditions created by action of the United Nations or otherwise, and shall so report to the Congress.

The House adopted the joint "Formosa Resolution" without change by 409–3 vote after only 3 hours of debate. The Senate Foreign Relations and Armed Services committees jointly approved the resolution Jan. 26 by 27–2 vote; those voting against the resolution were Wayne Morse (independent, Ore.) and William Langer (R., N.D.). The vote followed 2 days of private hearings during which the Joint Chiefs of Staff were questioned. The committees turned down, 20–8, amendments offered by Sens. Hubert H. Humphrey (D., Minn.) and Estes Kefauver (D., Tenn.) to exclude

U.S. military commitments from the lesser islands off the Chinese mainland.

Morse told the Senate Jan. 26 that a threat of U.S. "aggression" and preventive war was implicit in the resolution. Minority leader William F. Knowland (R., Calif.) denounced Morse as leading the Communist world to believe the U.S. was ready to provoke an Asian war. Sen. Ralph E. Flanders (R., Vt.), announcing his opposition to the resolution Jan. 26 (he had approved it in committee), said "this is preventive war."

The Senate passed the resolution by 85–3 vote Jan. 28, and Eisenhower signed it Jan. 29 with the observation that he was "deeply gratified." Those who voted against the resolution in the Senate Jan. 28 were Herbert H. Lehman (D.-Lib., N.Y.), Langer and Morse. They had voiced concern that the wide scope of the resolution could result in a U.S. war with Communist China.

Eisenhower had issued a statement Jan. 27 to dispel fears that the emergency authority he sought was for a preventive war against Communist China. He emphasized that U.S. naval and air forces deployed in the Taiwan area were "designed purely for defensive purposes" and that any decision to use them for other purposes would be taken by the President alone. He reiterated at his weekly news conference Feb. 2 that his purpose was "honestly and hopefully to prevent war" by making it clear to the Communists that they could not attack Taiwan without resistance.

Before its vote Jan. 28, the Senate had rejected, 83–3, an amendment offered by Langer to forbid the sending of U.S. armed forces nearer than 12 miles from the Chinese mainland. Renewed amendments from Kefauver and Humphrey to exclude the offshore Quemoy and Matsu Islands from the protected area were also defeated, 75–11 and 74–13, respectively. Humphrey Jan. 29 offered a separate resolution expressing U.S. support for UN cease-fire action

in the Taiwan Straits area. The resolution was referred to
the Foreign Relations Committee.

UN Discusses Chinese Fighting

Toward the end of Jan. 1955 the Taiwan Straits crisis
was brought before the UN Security Council. Chief New
Zealand delegate Sir Leslie Knox Munro, president of the
Security Council for January, formally requested Jan. 28
(with U.S. and British support) that the Council take up
the question of a cease-fire between the 2 Chinese governments. Munro explained that New Zealand, as a country in
the Pacific, naturally viewed with alarm the hostilities in
the Taiwan Straits area. His country's sole aim, he said, was
to stop the fighting.

The Soviet delegation to the UN Jan. 30 made public
a proposed Security Council resolution to halt what it called
U.S. "aggression" against mainland China. The Soviet item
called for a cease-fire in the Taiwan Straits and the immediate
removal of U.S. armed forces from the area.

In a 7-hour meeting Jan. 31, the Security Council voted,
9–1 (Russia opposed, Nationalist China abstaining), to
make New Zealand's proposal for a cease-fire discussion
the first item on its agenda. It then voted, 9–1 (Nationalist
China opposed, Russia abstaining), for a New Zealand
resolution, strongly indorsed by French delegate Henri
Hoppenot, to invite Communist China to participate in this
discussion.

Nationalist Chinese delegate T. F. Tsiang protested that
it would be an "insult" to the Chinese people if the UN
called on the Communists to represent them. Tsiang, however, did not attempt to have the resolution on inviting
Communist China classified as a matter of substance (rather
than procedural), which would have made it subject to veto
by Nationalist China.

The Security Council Jan. 31 voted, 10–1 (Nationalist China opposed), to make the Soviet draft resolution condemning U.S. "aggression" against China the 2d item on the agenda. Soviet delegate Arkady A. Sobolev, arguing for the Soviet resolution, assailed the New Zealand plan as a "clumsy maneuver" to prevent Communist China's "liberation" of Taiwan and the Pescadores. U.S. Amb.-to-UN Henry Cabot Lodge denounced as "a preposterous cold war fraud" the Soviet charge that the U.S. was bent on aggression against Communist China.

After the passage of the New Zealand resolutions, the Council adjourned to await an official Communist Chinese reply to the UN invitation, which Secy. Gen. Hammarskjöld cabled to Peking immediately following the adoption of the Security Council resolution.

The desirability of an immediate cease-fire and the straits crisis itself had already become matters for political debate in Britain. British Foreign Secy. Anthony Eden said in Parliament Jan. 26 that the UN would not ask the Communist Chinese to give up "what they regard as their rights" in the Far East crisis. British Labor Party leader Clement R. Attlee said Jan. 31 that: (a) the U.S. should abandon the idea that Taiwan was part of its Pacific defense ring; (b) Pres. Chiang Kai-shek and his chief Nationalist officials should be exiled from Taiwan; (c) Taiwan's people should decide by plebiscite whether they wanted to join Communist China.

In a Parliamentary debate Feb. 1, Prime Min. Sir Winston Churchill rejected Laborite demands that Taiwan be given to the Communists under the terms of the Cairo Declaration of Dec. 1, 1943. (The Declaration, signed by Churchill, Pres. Franklin D. Roosevelt and Chiang Kai-shek, declared that Taiwan should be returned to China after World War II.) Churchill said that the future sovereignty of Taiwan was left undetermined by the Japanese peace treaty.

Indian Prime Min. Jawaharlal Nehru, arriving in London

Jan. 29 to attend the first British Commonwealth Prime Ministers' Conference, proclaimed that India was ready "to play a peaceful role" in the Taiwan Straits crisis. Nehru met with Eden Jan. 30, and they reportedly discussed a conference Nehru had held with Communist Chinese Amb.-to-India Yuan Chung-hsin a few days previously.

Sir William G. Hayter, British ambassador to the USSR, had asked Soviet Foreign Min. Vyacheslav M. Molotov Jan. 28 to use Moscow's influence with Communist China to prevent any incident that might lead to "general hostilities" in the Far East. Molotov replied informally Jan. 28 that international tension would be lessened if the U.S. would "cease its aggressive actions in the area of Formosa." In a formal answer to Hayter's plea Jan. 31, Molotov said that he had passed on to Communist China the British and New Zealand views that a cease-fire was necessary to prevent the outbreak of a major war. Molotov said that Russia was "alarmed by the dangerous situation" in the Taiwan Straits. He again blamed the U.S. and Chiang Kai-shek for the crisis.

(Molotov returned to the matter Feb. 8 in an extensive foreign policy review to the Supreme Soviet in Moscow. He said: "Taiwan and the Pescadores, not to mention the other off-shore islands, are indisputably the territory of China. . . . Notwithstanding this, these islands have been seized by the U.S.A., which maintains there Chiang Kai-shek's criminal gang. . . . Recently matters have gone to such a length that the President and Congress of the United States. . .have openly started to threaten war against the Chinese people, who are upholding their rights to these islands and are defending their national honor and sovereignty. . . . We consider the Taiwan question to be a domestic affair of China's and regard the predatory actions of the U.S.A., and its threat of war, as aggression that must be condemned unreservedly by the United Nations if it prizes its authority. It is no longer possible to tolerate a situation where the legitimate rights of China in the UN have not yet been restored because of opposition by the United States. The U.S.A. must withdraw from Taiwan and the Taiwan Straits all its armed forces, including air and naval forces. Then hostilities in the Far East will cease and peace will be established. . . ."

(Molotov denounced as one of several "military and political blocs and aggressive groupings" formed by Washington "the treaty between the U.S.A. and the bankrupt Chiang Kai-shek." Molotov included Communist China among the countries with which Soviet relations were developing "on the basis of fraternal friendship and over-all cooperation" and which, together with the USSR, comprised "a monolithic camp of peace, democracy and socialism." The Soviet Union, he said, was "bound to the great People's Republic of China by ties of friendship and fraternal relations that are growing stronger from year to year.")

Communist China was cool to the UN invitation to take part in the Security Council's cease-fire discussion. A statement broadcast from Peking Jan. 29, 2 days before the Security Council's resolution, included Premier-Foreign Min. Chou En-lai's advance rejection of a Taiwan Straits cease-fire. It asked the UN to "take steps to check U.S. aggression against China" and to force U.S. withdrawal from Taiwan and adjacent waters.

A Peking broadcast Jan. 31 reported a cabinet resolution and statements from leaders of mainland China's 3 "independent" parties (Li Chi-shen of the Revolutionary Kuomintang, Chiang Lan of the Democratic League and Chang Po-chun of the Farmers & Workers), all denouncing any Taiwan Straits cease-fire. Peking radio also rejected Clement R. Attlee's Taiwan "neutralization" proposal of Jan. 31. The Jan. 31 broadcast again accused the U.S. of "attempting to use the threat of atomic weapons" against Communist China. It asserted the Chinese Communists' confidence that they would quickly master atomic techniques.

Peking Feb. 3, 1955 officially sent the UN a message

refusing its invitation to attend the Security Council discussions of the Taiwan Straits warfare except on this condition: that Nationalist China's representative be "driven out from the Security Council" and the mainland government receive China's seat.

Chou En-lai notified UN Secy. Gen. Hammarskjöld in the Feb. 3 note that his government then would take part in a Security Council discussion of U.S. "acts of aggression" in the Taiwan area. Chou contended that Taiwan and the Pescadores were Chinese territory and that U.S. aid to the Nationalists in holding them was "intervention in China's internal affairs." Chou demanded that the Security Council "condemn the U.S. for its acts of aggression against China." He declared that Security Council actions taken with the Nationalists representing China were "null and void." He said his régime would support all "genuine international efforts to ease and eliminate the tension" over China.

New Zealand's proposal that the UN Security Council try to arrange for a cease-fire in the Taiwan area was tabled by the Council Feb. 14. The Council's efforts came to a halt because the Chinese Communists had refused to join the discussions unless they received the Council seat held by the Chinese Nationalists.

Discussion Feb. 14 produced tacit agreement among the majority of delegates that there was no alternate plan of procedure at hand. Henri Hoppenot of France said that truce talks would be useless with Communist China absent. He suggested that the impasse might be broken through channels of "traditional diplomacy." Soviet delegate Arkady A. Sobolev declared that it would be "impossible to solve international problems, especially in the Far East, without the participation of [Communist] China." Nationalist Chinese delegate T. F. Tsiang protested that the Council should "muster enough courage to face the basic and monstrous fact of the aggression of international communism in the Far East." But the Council adjourned indefinitely with New

Zealand's truce-making proposal still pending. U.S. Amb.-to-UN Henry Cabot Lodge said later that the Council had "not concluded" its consideration of New Zealand's plan but rather "has hardly begun" to consider it.

The Council rejected by 10–1 vote Feb. 14 a Soviet demand that it take up immediately a Soviet resolution to condemn alleged American "acts of aggression...against the People's Republic of China."

USSR Proposes International Conference

When it became apparent that the UN Security Council would be unable to deal with the Taiwan Straits crisis, the Soviet Union took the initiative of proposing a new forum outside the framework of the world organization.

Worldwide press reports Feb. 2–7 indicated that the USSR had proposed through contacts with Britain and India a non-UN conference on a cease-fire for China's off-shore area. U.S. and British Commonwealth leaders were said Feb. 7–8 to have rejected such a plan although the Commonwealth group sought to arrange an unwritten off-shore truce.

The Soviet government Feb. 12 made public its plan for a 10-power, non-UN conference about Taiwan and the off-shore islands. The Nationalist Chinese would be excluded from such a conference. The plan had been suggested by the USSR to Britain Feb. 4 in a note proposing a conference in February in Shanghai or New Delhi attended by the U.S., the USSR, Communist China, Britain, France, India, Burma, Indonesia, Pakistan and Ceylon. The Soviet note said that the U.S. and Britain had maneuvered in the Security Council to obstruct mainland China's "just and lawful" possession of Taiwan and that Russia, in demanding UN condemnation of American "aggressive actions" toward Taiwan, strove for "the strengthening of peace in the Far East."

The British Foreign Office said Feb. 12 that it had answered the Soviet note by (a) questioning whether a conference excluding either Chinese régime could have a "useful result," (b) asserting that any conference concerning Taiwan should be "organized in a form acceptable to the UN," and (c) urging that all powers try to "stop the fighting in the area" and "reduce the risk" of dangerous incidents. Britain indicated that most prime ministers of other Commonwealth countries who earlier had conferred in London, had approved of the reply.

U.S. diplomatic officials declined comment on the Moscow-London exchange of notes but let it be known that they also approved of Britain's reply. Britain said it had "informed" the U.S. of Russia's offer.

The possibility of working out plans for an international conference on the Taiwan Straits crisis was said to have been discussed again when P. N. Kaul, Indian chargé d'affaires in Moscow, called on Soviet Foreign Min. Vyacheslav M. Molotov Feb. 14.

Reports from London Feb. 14 said Indian Prime Min. Jawaharlal Nehru and British Foreign Secy. Sir Anthony Eden had asked Premier Chou En-lai for an informal promise that his régime would not use force to take Nationalist-held islands near the mainland. Nehru was said to believe that the Nationalists would soon evacuate all islands except Taiwan and the Pescadores if the Communists stopped attacking them.

U.S. Restrains Chiang and Warns Peking

Under the mutual defense pact of 1955, the U.S. was committed to defend Taiwan and the Pescadores. The offshore islands then under the Chinese Nationalist occupation were not explicitly covered by the defense pact.

Nationalist Chinese Foreign Min. George K. C. Yeh said Feb. 11, after a talk with U.S. Assistant State Secy. (for Far Eastern affairs) Walter S. Robertson, that the U.S.

would help defend "all the offshore islands." But he amended this in a statement in San Francisco while en route home Feb. 11 and said that such a course of action was a "possibility," a matter "for the U.S. to decide." Nationalist Pres. Chiang Kai-shek told newsmen in Taipei Feb. 14 that he thought U.S.-Nationalist plans for joint defense of the offshore islands were "quite clear" and that all military experts regarded Quemoy and Matsu as "essential" to the defense of Taiwan and the Pescadores. According to press reports Feb. 14, an "informed" U.S. source had said: no promise to defend Quemoy and Matsu had been made to the Nationalists, but their capture by the Communists would mean the loss of Nationalist garrisons totaling about ⅓ of the National army (300,000 to 400,000 men).

U.S. State Secy. Dulles made these points in a speech at a Foreign Policy Association dinner in New York Feb. 16: the U.S. was not obligated to defend the off-shore islands "as such," but it would "assure that Taiwan and the Pescadores will not be forcibly taken over by the Communists"; Communist Chinese propagandists had indicated Peking's intention to take Taiwan, "and they treat the coastal islands as means to that end"; U.S. action would depend on "subsequent Chinese Communist actions."

In the meantime, the Nationalist Chinese on Taiwan, after some consultation with Washington, had evacuated the Tachen Islands. The removal of 10,000 Nationalist army troops, 4,000 guerrillas, 14,500 civilians and 9,857 tons of ammunition and other cargo from the Tachen Islands was completed Feb. 11 by the U.S. 7th Fleet and supporting U.S. Air Force units. The evacuées' transfer to Taiwan was finished Feb. 13. The Communist Chinese, who made no attempt to interfere with the evacuation, announced Feb. 14 that they had taken over the Tachens, which the retiring Nationalists left barren. The 7th Fleet resumed its normal patrol of Taiwan Straits Feb. 12, and the U.S. Far East Air Force retained a squadron of Sabrejets on assignment to Taiwan. The Nationalists announced Feb. 14 the evacuation of 2,000 civilians from Nank, an island 80 miles south of the Tachens.

The evacuation of the Tachen Islands was followed by more armed clashes between the Communist and Nationalist Chinese. Chinese Nationalist bombers and naval craft claimed major victories Feb. 18–22 in strikes against mainland Chinese convoys converging on Communist-held Taishan (Tai Island) some 130 miles northwest of Taiwan and roughly midway between Nationalist-held Nanchi (Nanchishan) and Matsu Islands.

The Nationalists said a submarine (nationality not specified), 8 landing craft (capacity: 200 troops each), 5 gunboats and 8 armed motorized junks were sunk Feb. 18 by Nationalist warships, joined later by planes, who attacked a Communist convoy. The Nationalists claimed to have damaged 2 other landing craft and 8 gunboats and to have destroyed 8 barracks and several supply dumps on Taishan. This was the biggest sea action since Nov. 1954 and the Nationalists' biggest victory since they were driven off the mainland in 1949. The Nationalists reported sinking 15 more Communist junks and damaging 5 as the battle resumed Feb. 19. Another Communist gunboat and several junks were reported destroyed Feb. 20, and a Communist boat and 5 junks were reported sunk Feb. 22.

State Secy. John Foster Dulles went to Taipei Mar. 3 to confer with Nationalist Pres. Chiang Kai-shek after a trip by Dulles to Bangkok, Thailand to attend a South East Asia Treaty Organization (SEATO Council meeting. Dulles urged a Taiwan Straits cease-fire, and Chiang reportedly rejected this advice. (Nationalist Foreign Min. George K. C. Yeh told the Legislative Yuan Mar. 15 that the Nationalist government would definitely defend the off-shore islands of Quemoy and Matsu.)

Dulles, back from his trip to the Far East, warned Communist China in a countrywide TV-and-radio broadcast from Washington Mar. 8 not to underestimate American willingness to meet a military challenge to Taiwan and other parts of the Far East whose defense the U.S. considered vital to non-Communist countries' security.

Dulles said that "the Allied powers possess plenty of strength" in the SEATO area and that an adequate defense did not require "large static forces at all points. The U.S. contribution will be primarily in terms of sea and air power." American sea and air forces "in this area" already were "equipped with new and powerful weapons of precision, which can utterly destroy military targets without endangering unrelated civilian centers," Dulles declared. He said he had told the SEATO allies at the conference in Bangkok that a new act of "open armed aggression" by Communist China "would probably mean that they have decided on general war in Asia." In this case, he pointed out, the Communist Chinese would have to cope with war on all fronts, taking into account U.S. mutual defense treaties with South Korea and Nationalist China. An attempt to wage war simultaneously in the South, Center and North "would strain their inadequate means of transportation." Dulles said the Seato Council had studied the "military factors" and was optimistic about Allied ability to turn back a Communist attack.

Dulles' broadcast remarks (similar to statements he had made to the Senate Foreign Relations Committee earlier Mar. 8) included an assertion that Congress' "Formosa Resolution" authorization of the President to take action necessary to defend Taiwan "did more than any other recent act to inspire our Asian friends with confidence in us." But he said that further demonstrations of American will to resist Communist Chinese aggression might be necessary.

Of the struggle between Taipei and Peking, Dulles said:

Let me make it clear that we have here to deal with 2 distinct matters—first, the political decision of what to defend, and then the decision as to how to defend it. The decision of what to defend has been taken. It is expressed in the treaty and also in the law whereby Congress has authorized the President to use the U.S. armed forces in the Formosa area. That decision is to defend Formosa and the Pescadores. However, the law permits a defense which will be flexible and not necessarily confined to a static defense of Formosa and the Pescadores themselves. How to implement this flexible defense Pres. Eisenhower will decide, in the light of his judgment as to the over-all value of certain coastal positions to the defense of Formosa, and the cost of holding these positions. And his judgment would take account of consultations provided for by the mutual defense treaty.

We hope that the present military activities of the Chinese Communists are not in fact the first stage of an attack against Formosa and the Pescadores. We hope that a cease-fire may be attainable. We know that friendly nations, on their own responsibility, are seeking to find substance for these hopes. Also, the UN is studying the matter in a search for peace. So far these efforts have not been rewarded by any success. The Chinese Communists seem to be determined to try to conquer Formosa. The response of the United States will have importance both to Formosa itself and to all the Southeast Asian and Pacific countries.

I come back from Asia greatly impressed by the spirit and the purpose of the governments and the peoples with whom I had contact. They want to preserve their freedom and independence. However, patriotism alone is not enough. Small nations cannot easily be self-confident when they are next door to Communist China. Its almost unlimited manpower would easily dominate, and could quickly engulf, the entire area were it not restrained by the mutual security structure which has been erected. But that structure will not hold if it be words alone. Essential ingredients are the deterrent power of the United States and our willingness to use that power in response to a military challenge. The Chinese Communists seem determined to make such a challenge.

At the same time they are persistently trying to belittle our power and throw doubt on our resolution. They boast that in 1950, in Korea, they drove U.S. forces back from the Yalu and gained a great victory. They boast of their victory over the French Union forces in Indochina at Dienbienphu, and they misrepresent our non-participation as due to our weakness of will. When we recently helped the Chinese Nationalists to evacuate the Tachens and other coastal islands, the Chinese Communists claimed that this represented great 'victories' for them. They continue wrongfully to hold our fliers and citizens. In such ways Chinese Communist propaganda portrays the U.S.A. as being merely a 'paper tiger.' It suggests to the small peoples whom they threaten that the U.S.A. will always find reasons to fall back when faced by brutal and uncompromising force and that Communist China is sure to win.

The United States, in the interests of peace, has made great sacrifices and has shown great self-restraint. That is nothing for which we should feel ashamed. Indeed, it is something in which we can take pride. But we must always remember that the free nations of the Western Pacific and Southeast Asia will quickly lose their freedom if they think that our love of peace means peace at any price. We must, if occasion offers, make it clear that we are prepared to stand firm and, if necessary, meet hostile force with the greater force that we possess.

A big step in the right direction was taken by the Congress when, at the President's request, it passed the joint resolution which authorized the President actually to use the U.S. armed forces for the defense of Formosa and, to the extent that the President judges appropriate for that defense, to protect related positions in friendly hands. That nonpartisan action, taken with virtual unanimity, did more than any other recent act to inspire our Asian friends with confidence in us. I believe that their confidence is not misplaced. . . .

Congress Divided on Offshore Islands

With the military situation in the Taiwan Straits continuing tense, there was much speculation in Washington about the possibility of war over Quemoy and Matsu. A high-ranking military source (later identified as Adm. Robert B. Carney, the chief of naval operations) was reported to have predicted Communist attack on Quemoy and Matsu after Apr. 15, 1955.

Discounting this prediction, Pres. Eisenhower said at his news conference Mar. 30 that he would not reprimand Carney. Eisenhower urged that the U.S. "be as fair and as large-minded as we know how to accommodate and to understand the fears and the ambitions of others that might lead them into a risky venture. . .at the same time so conducting ourselves that the world knows we are strong. . . ." He did not answer directly when asked whether the U.S. would defend Quemoy and Matsu against Communist attack but observed that maintenance of the morale and fighting spirit of the people and forces on Taiwan was a key element in the defense of Taiwan.

The President, aided by State Secy. Dulles, also began Mar. 30 a 2-day series of briefing sessions on the world situation with House and Senate leaders of both parties. House Speaker Sam Rayburn (D., Tex.) said after a session at the White House: "I don't feel any better," but "I won't tell you why." Chairman Carl Vinson (D., Ga.) of the House Armed Services Committee declared himself "in complete accord with everything" Dulles and the President "said about Asia."

Sen. Estes Kefauver (D., Tenn.) protested in a Senate speech Mar. 30 that the involvement of the U.S. in "a war over Matsu and Quemoy ought to be unthinkable," but, he charged, "there are those in high places in the present Administration itself who are plotting and planning to bring about such a war."

The controversy over the likelihood of a Communist attack on the offshore islands—and over whether the U.S. should risk general war to help repel it—provoked statements by the 2 party leaders in the U.S. Senate Mar. 28. Majority leader Lyndon Johnson (D., Tex.) accused right-wing Republicans of "talking war." He said the U.S. wanted neither a "war party" nor an "appeasement party." Minority leader William F. Knowland (R., Calif.), replying to Johnson, asked whether the Democrats wanted the U.S. to go "marching down the hill again in the face of Communist threats."

APPROACH TO NEGOTIATIONS (1955)

Chou Proposes Direct Talks with U.S.

Following the end of the Korean War, the U.S. and Communist China had maintained intermittent contact through talks in Panmunjom and—since 1954—in Geneva. These talks were considered singularly unproductive. As the spring of 1955 wore on, renewed interest in opening diplomatic negotiations was shown both in Washington and Peking. The U.S. government was concerned mainly with the release of American prisoners of war held in mainland China. The Communist Chinese objective was broader—the settlement of political questions. During the Bandung Conference of Afro-Asian countries, held in Apr. 1955, Communist Chinese Premier-Foreign Min. Chou En-lai took the initiative of proposing U.S.-Communist Chinese talks.

The Conference of Afro-Asian states, sponsored by the Colombo Conference countries (India, Burma, Ceylon and Indonesia), had opened Apr. 18 in Bandung, an Indonesian resort city southeast of Jakarta. Delegates from 29 Afro-Asian countries attended. The U.S. sent as an unofficial observer, Rep. Adam Clayton Powell Jr. (D., N.Y.).

The sponsor nations sought to avoid highly controversial topics, such as Taiwan and Israel, during formal conference sessions. Egypt, Iraq and Jordan failed Apr. 17 in an effort to place the Israeli question on the agenda. Their effort was resisted by Prime Mins. U Nu of Burma and Jawaharlal Nehru of India. But Communist Chinese Premier Chou En-lai told the conference's political committee Apr. 20 that he would support a resolution expressing Arab demands for territorial revisions in Palestine and permission for Arab refugees to return to Israel. Chou insisted, however, that references to the UN must be removed from this resolution and from one on human rights. Chou likened the Palestinian and Taiwanese issues to one another and held that

29

the Palestinian question could be settled once extrinsic factors causing the "Palestine tragedy" had ceased operating.

In an opening speech before the full conference Apr. 19, Chou had said that his Chinese mainland delegation had come to Bandung "to seek unity and not to quarrel." He continued: "Agreements on the restoration of peace in Indochina reached at the Geneva conference are endangered. The U.S. continues to create tension in the Taiwan area. Countries outside of Asia and Africa are establishing more and more military bases in Asian and African countries. They are creating more and more atomic weapons..." Chou said that the "will of the Chinese people to liberate Taiwan and the coastal islands is a just one." He accused the U.S. of carrying out subversive activities in his country "without disguise." Chou said most African and Asian countries, "including China, are still very backward economically owing to the long period of colonial domination. That is why we demand not only political independence but economic independence as well." He said that all countries, "big or small, strong or weak, should all enjoy equal rights in international relations. Their territorial integrity and sovereignty should not be violated."

(Chou added that his government was "willing to promote normalization of relations" with Japan and other Asian and African countries. He said that dual nationality of Chinese minorities in Southeast Asian countries was "something left behind by the old China" and that his government "is ready to solve the question" with the "governments of the countries concerned.")

Beyond these remarks, Chou went no further on the subject of Taiwan—until the matter was raised again by Ceylonese Prime Min. Sir John Kotelawala, who proposed Apr. 21 these 5 steps toward a settlement of the Taiwanese question: (a) the immediate transfer to Communist China of Quemoy and Matsu islands; (b) a complete withdrawal of the U.S. 7th Fleet from the Taiwan Straits; (c) the "honorable retirement" of Generalissimo Chiang Kai-shek; (d) a 5-year trusteeship over Taiwan, to be administered by either the UN or the Colombo Powers; and (e) at the end of that 5-year period, a plebiscite by the Taiwanese on whether Taiwan was to remain Chinese territory and join the mainland or to become independent.

Afterwards, Chou conferred with Kotelawala, with the government leaders of the other Colombo Powers—Burmese Prime Min. U Nu, Indian Prime Min. Nehru, Indonesian Premier Ali Sastroamidjojo and Pakistani Prime Min. Mohammed Ali—and with Gen. Carlos Romulo, ex-foreign minister of the Philippines, and Siamese Foreign Min. Prince Wan Waithayakon.

The bid for direct talks with the U.S. was made by Chou Apr. 23 in a short sentence that he released after his lunch with 8 leading Bandung Conference delegates. The statement read: "The Chinese people are friendly to the American people. The Chinese people do not want to have war with the U.S.A. The Chinese government is willing to sit down and enter into negotiations with the U.S. government to discuss the question of relaxing tension in the Far East and especially the question of relaxing tension in the Taiwan area."

That afternoon, speaking before the political committee of the Conference, Chou repeated this position, saying: "The Chinese people do not want to have war with the U.S. We are willing to settle international disputes by peaceful means." "If those of you here would like to facilitate the settlement of disputes between China and the U.S. by peaceful means, it would be most beneficial to the relaxation of tension in the Far East and also to the postponement and prevention of a world war."

Chou reiterated his plea for direct talks with the U.S. in a speech Apr. 24 at the closing of the Bandung Conference. He said: "China and the U.S. should sit down and enter into negotiation to settle the question of relaxing and eliminating the tension in the Taiwan area. However, this should not in the slightest degree affect the just demand of the Chinese people to exercise their sovereign rights in liberating Taiwan."

U.S. Response Cautious

Chou En-lai's statement of Apr. 23, 1955 reached the U.S. State Department while State Secy. Dulles was away on vacation. The department responded by issuing a statement of its own Apr. 23. The U.S., it said, would always welcome sincere efforts to secure peace. "If Communist China is sincere," it continued, "there are a number of obvious steps it could take [to] give evidence [of] its good intentions," such as: "to place in effect in the [Taiwan] area an immediate cease-fire"; "immediately release the American airmen and others whom it unjustly holds"; and accept "the outstanding invitation [of the UN Security] Council to participate in discussions to end hostilities in the Formosa region."

U.S. State Department officials said Apr. 24 that it was "up to Mr. Chou to formalize his proposal" for direct talks "by informing the U.S. officially, through the diplomatic channels of a 3d country that has relations with the U.S. and Communist China." They repeated that the Nationalist Chinese must be present at such talks.

Peking radio scored the State Department Apr. 26 for "hastily. . .putting forth unreasonable prerequisites" for a "necessary" U.S.-Communist Chinese meeting to discuss "the tense situation arising from U.S. intervention" in the Taiwan situation.

The U.S. modified its position when Dulles returned to Washington from vacation. At his press conference Apr. 26 Dulles said: "The first thing is to find out whether there is a possibility of a cease-fire in the area. That is a matter which can be discussed, perhaps bilaterally, or at the UN, or possibly under other circumstances. But I regard a cease-fire as the indispensable prerequisite to anything further. When you get into further matters, then the interests of the Chinese Nationalists would naturally come to play a very large part."

Dulles added that the U.S. "does not negotiate with a pistol aimed at its head." He said Chou may have been "playing a propaganda game" in proposing talks with the U.S., "but we intend to try to find out. In doing so, we shall not, of course, depart from the path of fidelity and honor toward our ally," Nationalist China. Dulles said he had not seen or approved the State Department statement of Apr. 23. The statement had been drafted under the direction of State Undersecy. Herbert Hoover Jr. and cleared by phone with Pres. Eisenhower, who was at his Gettysburg farm.

Eisenhower said at his press conference Apr. 27 that he agreed with Dulles. "I believe it is perfectly legitimate for us to talk to the Chincoms [Chinese Communists] about stopping firing." He added that "if we overstated the case Saturday [Apr. 23], well, that was to that extent an error in terminology." He said the Apr. 23 statement "may have erred in not being as complete as it should have been, but I don't believe it was a reversal of attitude." The President pointed out that Dulles had made it clear "we would not discuss the affairs of the Chinese Nationalists behind their back, but. . . as a test of good intent, if the Chinese Communists wanted to talk merely about cease-fire, we would be glad to meet with them and talk with them." Eisenhower said the U.S. would talk with Communist China about "anything that doesn't affect the Chinese Nationalists" if "there seems to be an opportunity for us to further the easing of tensions, the advancement of world peace, and certainly getting back our prisoners."

The reaction on Capitol Hill was mixed. Chairman Walter F. George (D., Ga.) of the Senate Foreign Relations

Committee said Apr. 23 that he thought Chou's mind had been opened by what "he saw and witnessed" at the Bandung Conference. "We ought to be willing to talk with" the Communist Chinese "because we certainly owe a high obligation to all mankind everywhere," George said.

Senate majority leader Lyndon B. Johnson (D., Tex.) said Apr. 25 that he hoped Sen. George's statement "will receive the careful consideration of every policy-making official of our government." Johnson added, however, that Communist talk about "liberating" Taiwan cast doubt on the Communists' sincerity. George declined to comment Apr. 25 on whether Chou's remark Apr. 24 about "liberating" Taiwan had changed his views. But he said the Nationalist Chinese would "have to be represented directly or indirectly" if "we were going to dispose of any of their contentions or rights."

Sen. Estes Kefauver (D., Tenn.) praised George's initiative and proposed that the U.S. open talks with its allies on a "just settlement" in the Far East. Sen. John J. Sparkman (D., Ala.) said Communist sincerity could best be tested by renewing UN efforts for a Taiwan Straits cease-fire.

Senate minority leader William F. Knowland (R., Calif.) voiced strong opposition to Chou's bid. He said Apr. 27 that the Communist Chinese "don't need a conference to bring about a cease-fire. All they need is to stop shooting and building up their aggressive forces" in the Taiwan Straits area. The State Department's Apr. 23 statement, Knowland said, "seemed consistent with our long-established policy of expecting deeds rather than words as a prelude to another conference."

Knowland in his Apr. 27 statement made no mention of either Eisenhower's or Dulles' statement. He said: "Unless there is some formula regarding which I have not been advised and which is difficult for me to now envision, I find it hard to comprehend how we could enter into direct negotiations with Communist China without the interests of the Republic of China being deeply involved."

At a New York press conference Apr. 25, Knowland had restated his position that the U.S. should help defend Quemoy and Matsu Islands. He made this counter-proposal to suggestions that Taiwan be placed under UN trusteeship: "Why don't the appeasers suggest a division of mainland China at the Yangtze River" and, after 10 years, a UN plebiscite on Communist or Nationalist rule?

12 Republican U.S. Senators Apr. 30 issued a statement supporting Eisenhower's stand on Taiwan Straits cease-fire talks with Communist China. The 12 asserted that the President "has a right and obligation to wage peace as well as to wage war. Waging peace is what he is trying to do." The statement, prepared by Sen. Clifford P. Case (R., N.J.), was signed by Sens. Gordon Allott (Colo.), J. Glenn Beall (Md.), Prescott Bush (Conn.), Frank Carlson (Kan.), Norris Cotton (N.H.), James H. Duff (Pa.), Irving M. Ives (N.Y.), Thomas H. Kuchel (Calif.), Frederick G. Payne (Me.), Leverett Saltonstall (Mass.) and H. Alexander Smith (N.J.). Saltonstall and Smith, in a supplementary statement, said it would be "most advisable, if possible," to include Nationalist China in the proposed talks.

The 12 Senators' statement was regarded as a repudiation by them of the Taiwan policy advocated by Knowland. Knowland said Apr. 30 that he had "no present intention of resigning" in protest against the Administration's Far Eastern policies.

Sen. Ralph E. Flanders (R., Vt.) said Apr. 30 that Knowland was an "excellent" floor leader, "with emphasis on the word 'floor,'" but it was "very unfortunate that he expresses himself so strongly about Formosa."

Democratic leader Adlai E. Stevenson, in Salisbury, Southern Rhodesia on a business trip, said Apr. 30 that he was "very glad" to hear of the Administration's attitude toward Chou's offer to confer with the U.S., which Stevenson had called "very heartening." Stevenson observed: "When you refuse to get together and talk, that is when shooting starts."

Radford & Robertson Go to Taiwan

Pres. Eisenhower sent Adm. Arthur W. Radford, chairman of Joint Chiefs of Staff, and Walter S. Robertson, Assistant State Secretary for Far Eastern Affairs, to confer with Pres. Chiang Kai-shek. Radford and Robertson left Washington Apr. 20, 1955. They conferred with Chiang at Taipei Apr. 24–Apr. 27 and reported to Eisenhower May 3 on their talks. The contents of their report were not disclosed, but Radford told newsmen afterwards that the U.S. would probably increase its 900-man military assistance mission on Taiwan. He would neither confirm nor deny a report (in the *N.Y. Times* Apr. 30) that the U.S. would base a token military force on Taiwan to bolster Nationalist Chinese morale.

The Nationalist government on Taiwan May 1 issued a formal denial of Washington reports that Chiang had agreed to a cease-fire if Peking were willing. In a message marking the establishment of the (Nationalist) Chinese Association for Psychological Warfare May 1, Chiang Kai-shek urged that the group "hasten the downfall of the Communist puppets and recover the mainland." He called the Taiwan Straits situation tense.

Progress Toward Parley

Chou En-lai's call for talks with the U.S. gave rise to a good deal of diplomatic activity on the part of 3d countries.

Pakistani Prime Min. Mohammed Ali discussed Taiwan with Chou in Bandung Apr. 25, 1955 and later told newsmen that he had suggested to Chou the release of 11 U.S. airmen as a gesture toward "eliminating suspicion on both sides."

Ali did not give Chou's reply but said that Communist China "might release them if convinced that the U.S. is anxious to bring about a peaceful settlement." Ali said Chou "showed every desire" for a peaceful settlement but had regarded the State Department statement of Apr. 23 as a "rebuff."

British Foreign Secy. Harold Macmillan told the British House of Commons Apr. 27 that he had instructed Humphrey Trevelyan, British chargé d'affaires in Peking, to ask Chou to amplify his offer to negotiate with the U.S. Macmillan denied that Britain had made any commitment to join the U.S. in defending Taiwan.

Indian Prime Min. Jawaharlal Nehru announced to his parliament Apr. 30 that V. K. Krishna Menon, the Indian UN delegate, had been invited to Peking by Chou En-lai to continue discussions of "certain aspects" of the Taiwan situation that they had begun during the Bandung Conference. Nehru said that the Indian government had canvassed the "reactions and attitude" of the U.S., Britain and Canada on the Taiwan issue and would strive to avert "the grim alternative that faces us if there are to be no negotiations." Menon, who planned to complete his Peking trip during May before Nehru visited Moscow in June, said May 2 in New Delhi that he would try to reconcile U.S.-Communist Chinese differences.

Pres. Eisenhower said at his news conference May 4 that there had been no progress toward cease-fire talks with the Chinese Communists. He said that "we are sort of in a wait-and-see attitude" with a "number of countries. . .conducting explorations." Asked how the U.S. could distinguish between a Communist attack on only Quemoy and Matsu Islands and one that might pose the threat of an assault on Taiwan, the President said that it would depend on the type and amount of material used in the attack. The U.S. was pledged to the defense of Taiwan, but no commitment was made on the coastal islands, he said.

The first sign of progress in the effort by diplomatic intermediaries appeared with the release of 4 American airmen who had been held prisoners in mainland China for more than 2 years. They were "deported" May 31 to Hong Kong. All of them had been jet pilots shot down in the Korean War. They were: Lt. Col. Edwin Heller, 36, of Wynnewood, Pa.; Capt. Harold Fischer Jr., 28, of Swea City, Ia.; First Lt. Roland W. Parks, 24, of Omaha, Neb. and First Lt. Lyle Cameron, 26, of Lincoln, Neb.

According to the Hsinhua (New China) News Agency, the 4 airmen had been tried May 24 before a 3-man military tribunal, "the Supreme People's Court," and found guilty of "intruding into China's territorial air ... to conduct harassing and provocative activities." The announcement said that the airmen were released because they "were only carrying out. . . orders. . . and have all admitted their crimes and expressed remorse." "They are therefore being treated with leniency."

The first public announcement of their release came May 30 from Indian diplomat V. K. Krishna Menon, who had returned to New Delhi May 24 after an 11-day visit to Peking for talks with Chou En-lai. Menon said that Chou's government still held the 11 U.S. airmen convicted of espionage and sabotage in Nov. 1954 because they were considered to be in a different category.

Responding to the new development, Pres. Eisenhower said at his news conference May 31: "Our messages from various sources" indicated that the Chinese Communists released the 4 fliers as "a token on their part to do something in helping release tensions. But I must say that everything that happens in the world these days has to be studied, examined and. . . more carefully watched than would be implied in just a hit-or-miss guess as to what it means at this moment."

Menon left New Delhi June 1 for London en route to Washington, to suggest ways of "lowering tensions" between the U.S. and Communist China. He had said May 30 that Chou's government would be willing to talk with Chiang Kai-shek at the proper time but on an internal, not an international, basis. En route, Menon conferred with British officials in London June 3–8, Canadian officials in Ottawa June 9 and UN Secy. Gen. Dag Hammarskjöld at the UN Secretariat in New York June 11.

Pres. Eisenhower, Vice Pres. Richard M. Nixon and State Secy. John Foster Dulles conferred with Menon in Washington June 14. Nixon told newsmen that Menon "seemed to think substantial progress is being made toward the release of more [American] prisoners by the Chinese Communists" and that Menon was "optimistic about a continuation of the *de facto* cease-fire that is now in effect in the Formosan area." Nixon added that Menon had described the people of Communist China as "basically friendly" toward the American people.

Chou En-lai meanwhile acknowledged the rôle of the 3d countries in bringing the U.S. and Communist China to a conference. Chou told Indonesian newsmen in Peking June 2 (as reported by Peking radio June 10) that "China welcomes the rendering of good offices" by countries concerned about the Taiwan Straits situation, "especially those countries friendly to China." He again expressed willingness to "sit down and negotiate" with the U.S. to "ease and eliminate tension." "But since there is no war between China and the U.S., the question of a cease-fire does not arise," he said. "Still less can it be used as a prerequisite for the negotiation." He warned that "if there should be participation and inter-vention by foreign armed forces [in the Taiwan Straits area], international conflict would result, and that is precisely what we have always opposed."

Embassy-Level Talks Announced

The U.S. and Communist China announced July 25 that the talks going on between them in Geneva since 1954 would be raised from the consular to the ambassadorial level, effective Aug. 1, 1955. U.S. State Department officials said that the agreement resulted from mediation by the British chargé d'affaires in Peking, Douglas Walter O'Neill, and from suggestions by the Indian and Burmese governments.

The State Department's announcement said that the talks would be resumed at the ambassadorial level "in the hope that this would bring about agreement on the return of U.S. civilians detained in China and facilitate further discussions and settlement of other practical matters." Officials explained that no mention was made of U.S. airmen held in China because that subject was considered to be primarily under UN jurisdiction, although the U.S. would press for the airmen's release.

U.S. Amb.-to-Czechoslovakia U. Alexis Johnson, who began the U.S.-Chinese negotiations in Geneva, was to resume the talks, which the State Department said "do not involve diplomatic recognition." Peking announced July 27 that it would send its ambassador to Poland, Wang Ping-nan.

U.S. State Secy. Dulles said at his news conference July 26 that the U.S. was "primarily concerned" with the American civilians detained in Communist China, but "we shall hope to find out...whether the Chinese Communists accept the concept of a cease-fire" in the Taiwan Straits area in accordance with UN principles. Dulles said that the Chinese "no doubt" will have "matters of their own to bring up." The U.S. "will be disposed to discuss them" if they "directly involve the U.S. and Communist China." Dulles repeated a pledge of U.S. "fidelity and honor to our ally," Nationalist China.

Pres. Eisenhower said at his news conference July 27 that the talks might "eventually" reach the foreign ministers' level, as was suggested July 24 by Senate Foreign Relations Committee Chairman Walter F. George (D., Ga.). George had said (on NBC-TV's "Meet the Press") that the "quiescent" situation in the Taiwan Straits was "almost certain" to degenerate into an "acute flare-up" unless the U.S. agreed to a foreign ministers' conference with "the Soviet Chinese."

Shortly before the ambassadorial talks started Aug. 1 at the Hotel Beau Rivage in Geneva, Peking radio announced that the 11 U.S. fliers held since Nov. 1954 had been released July 31 and would reach Hong Kong Aug. 4.

Communist Chinese envoy Wang Ping-nan started the talks by confirming the fliers' release "in accordance with Chinese legal procedures." He expressed hope that it "will have favorable effects on our present talks." Wang said he was "convinced that with our joint efforts, it should be possible" to ease tensions between Washington and Peking. "So long as both of us adopt the attitude of negotiation and conciliation, there should not be any difficulty for us to reach a reasonable settlement" on the repatriation of civilians, Wang said.

Chinese High Hopes for Talks

Communist Chinese Premier Chou En-lai had voiced optimism concerning the ambassadorial talks before they opened in Geneva. In a speech to the National People's Congress July 30, Chou said that the Geneva talks should lead to "a reasonable settlement" on civilian repatriation. "The number of American civilians in China is small, and their question can be easily settled," he said. "The Chinese people are also concerned about the extremely unjust policy of blockade and embargo which obstructs trade between countries. It should be possible to remove such barriers so that peaceful trade between all countries will not be hindered."

Chou said that his government would try to make the Geneva talks "pave the way for further negotiations between

China and the U.S." "However, if anybody should take our efforts as a sign of weakness or imagine that pressure or threats will have effect on us, he will...quickly find out that his calculations are totally wrong." He said: "After the Korean armistice and the restoration of peace in Indochina, the situation in the Taiwan area has become the most tense in the Far East." This had been caused "by the U.S. occupation of China's territory, Taiwan, and its interference with the liberation of China's coastal islands." It was "an international issue between China and the U.S.," but the "exercise by the Chinese people of their sovereign rights in liberating Taiwan is a matter of China's internal affairs. Those 2 questions cannot be mixed."

Chou again rejected the suggestion of a cease-fire in the Taiwan Straits, again pointing out that there was no war between the U.S. and China. "So the question of cease-fire between China and the U.S. does not arise," he repeated. Chou indicated his wishes for direct talks with the Nationalist Chinese on Taiwan. He said: "Provided that the U.S. does not interfere with China's internal problems, the possibility of peaceful liberation of Taiwan will continue to increase. If possible, the Chinese government is willing to enter into negotiations with the responsible local authorities of Taiwan to map out concrete steps for Taiwan's peaceful liberation. It should be made clear that there should be negotiations between the central government and local authorities. The Chinese people are firmly opposed to any ideas or plots of the so-called '2 Chinas.'"

Washington Hopeful

The 11 U.S. fliers who had been kept prisoner in mainland China on charges of spying were released July 31, the day after Chou delivered his speech before the National People's Congress. On learning of this, State Secy. Dulles Aug. 1 issued a statement saying that the airmen's release resulted from "the patient course which the President has advocated, and which the country has supported." Pres. Eisenhower said: "The U.S. extends thanks to all who have contributed to this humanitarian result," particularly UN Secy. Gen. Dag Hammarskjöld.

Dulles appeared equally pleased with Chou's speech. He said at his news conference Aug. 2 that the speech indicated that Chou was "going further in the renunciation of force than anything he had said before." "What we hope to arrive at by progressive steps is a situation where the Chinese Communists will have renounced the use of force to achieve their ambitions," Dulles said. He added: "If they want to use force. . . that will almost surely start up a war, the limits of which could not be defined in advance."

"The release of the fliers, the release of the civilians—if it comes about—such statements as are made by Chou En-lai, if I interpret them right and if they are sincere and permanent parts of policy, might mark the beginning of a new phase in Chinese Communist relations with the rest of the world," Dulles declared. He said he hoped the Johnson-Wang talks "and the whole trend of world events" would create a situation in which "we can feel that we are not under the threat of war" in the Taiwan Straits area. He recalled his Apr. 26 remark about the U.S. being unwilling to negotiate with a pistol at its head and noted indications "that the pistol had been laid down." "But the important thing is that the pistol should be permanently discarded," Dulles added.

In the U.S. Senate, Sen. Joseph R. McCarthy (R., Wis.) July 28 introduced a resolution insisting on Chinese Nationalist participation in the Wang-Johnson talks. He engaged in a sharp Senate-floor exchange with Foreign Relations Committee Chairman Walter F. George (D., Ga.) in an attempt to get George's committee to act on the resolution before Congress adjourned. When George said the resolution would be considered "in order," McCarthy suggested George would be open to blame for a "deliberate attempt to bottle up" the resolution. (The committee adjourned July 30 without acting on the resolution.)

On the Senate floor Aug. 1, McCarthy said it was certain that the Russians had demanded that Quemoy and Matsu Islands be surrendered to the Chinese Communists and, "in view of today's news that the Chinese Communists have released 11 of the remaining 477 American prisoners of war, it is possible that this week's ambassadorial talks will simply ratify a deal made at the Big 4 meeting to surrender the off-shore islands to the Communists."

Senate minority leader William F. Knowland (R., Calif.) said: "No deal has been made to exchange the off-shore islands for American prisoners. I deny on behalf of the Administration, on the very highest authority,. . . that we are selling out or trading out our Asian allies or that we will negotiate their sovereignty or their independence or their people in any such nefarious deal."

U.S. Airmen Charge Torture

The 11 U.S. airmen released from Chinese Communist imprisonment arrived Aug. 4 in Hong Kong, where they received medical checkups, new clothing, food and back pay before taking off 6 hours later for Manila, en route to the U.S. All were reported to be in good health after 30 months' imprisonment, but Maj. William H. Baumer used crutches because of a leg wound and frostbite that had hospitalized him for 8 months. They had bailed out of a B-29 leaflet plane Jan. 12, 1953 after it was attacked by MIGs over North Korea.

Col. John Knox Arnold Jr., spokesman for the group, told newsmen in Tokyo Aug. 7 that he had been "subjected to types of persuasion that civilized people don't subject other people to." He said he was in solitary confinement for the full 30 months, except when taken to pose for pictures with other PWs (prisoners of war). The Communists, Arnold said, centered their punishment on him: he was punched, beaten with sticks and forced to stand with his legs tied together for 6 days, he said. He also described "a one-piece thing that went around the wrists," cutting off circulation. Guards would pull his fingers, "causing great pain clear up into my shoulders." The others experienced some physical ill-treatment but suffered mainly from intensive questioning and solitary confinement.

Arnold said he finally signed a "confession" that the B-29 "possibly" came down in Communist China. All the rest, except Baumer, signed similar statements after seeing his. Arnold said he tried to repudiate this statement at the trial.

Arnold had told newsmen Aug. 4 in Hong Kong that he and his comrades had learned that they were in Chinese hands 4 days after their capture. They were told they were PWs and would be treated in accordance with the Geneva Convention, he said, but he was not placed in a regular PW camp. All were taken to China 4 or 5 days after capture. Arnold said he was questioned during the first 8 months and spent the next 11 months in a cell. The Chinese did not accuse the fliers of having flown over China until Jan. 16, 1954. They were not told of espionage charges against them until just before their trial Oct. 10, 1954.

AMBASSADORIAL TALKS (1955-6)

The U.S.-Communist Chinese ambassadorial talks in Geneva opened Aug. 1, 1955 in an induced atmosphere of high expectations. Within 6 weeks, the talks produced an agreement on the repatriation of civilians. But thereafter, the talks made no progress.

Agenda; Peking Seeks Return of Students

At their first meeting, held Aug. 1, the 2 ambassadors— U. Alexis Johnson of the U.S. and Wang Ping-nan of Communist China—agreed on the following items to be included in the agenda of the talks:

(1) The return of civilians of both sides to their countries.

(2) Other practical matters at issue between the 2 governments.

The 2d item, inserted at the request of Wang encompassed a wide range of unspecified issues.

Communist China proposed that the ambassadorial talks be devoted to such basic issues in U.S.-Communist Chinese relations as the withdrawal of American troops from the Taiwan Straits and the establishment of trade and diplomatic relations. The U.S., on the other hand, was reluctant to be drawn into the discussion of these matters, its main concern being with more immediate objectives: the securing of a cease-fire in the Taiwan Straits and the release of U.S. citizens detained in Communist China.

At the outset of their talks, Johnson and Wang agreed that they should conduct their talks in private and not resort to publicity except through mutual agreement.

At their 2d meeting, held Aug. 2, Johnson and Wang exchanged lists of American civilians in mainland China. Johnson listed 40 Americans as jailed, under house arrest or denied exit permits. Wang's longer list included Americans who had expressed a desire to stay in Communist China.

47

Peking was seeking the return of more than 4,000 Chinese who had gone to the U.S. as students after World War II and had failed to return to their homeland after the Communists took over the Chinese mainland in 1949. U.S. screening, completed following the outbreak of the Korean War, had disclosed that about 124 of these Chinese had acquired skills of potential value to Communist China, and they were barred from leaving the U.S. Subsequently, an investigation conducted early in 1955 showed that 76 of this group wished to return to mainland China. In April they received permission to do so. The U.S. position in the Geneva talks was that all the Chinese (some no longer students) were free to leave the U.S. after April.

U.S. State Secy. John Foster Dulles, at a Washington news conference Aug. 2, categorically denied that the U.S. was keeping these Chinese from returning to China. Dulles said that he did not know whether financial difficulties had prevented the return of some of the Chinese, "but as far as any legal impediments are concerned, I can say categorically that there are none."

Wang proposed to Johnson Aug. 2 that a 3d power be allowed to verify the U.S. contention that some Chinese did not wish to return to mainland China. The talks were then adjourned until Aug. 4 to allow the 2 ambassadors to consult their respective governments.

U.S. State Department officials said Aug. 2 that the U.S. had rejected the 3d-power proposal when it was made in June by V. K. Krishna Menon, India's roving ambassador. They said the 3d power would, in effect, be supplanting Nationalist Chinese diplomatic representatives in the U.S.

Accord on Civilian Repatriation

Ambassadors Johnson and Wang continued their talks in Geneva Aug. 4 and 8 without disclosing details. In a joint communiqué issued Aug. 8, they said they had agreed not to make individual public statements "in the interest of seriously seeking solutions" of the problems before them. They said their talks had dealt only with civilians, except for Wang's announcement Aug. 1 of the release of 11 U.S. fliers.

Progress was slow at first. U. S. State Secy. Dulles Aug. 16 expressed his disappointment that the talks had not as yet come to an agreement about the release of U.S. civilians.

This apparently had an effect on Peking's attitude. At the 13th meeting of the ambassadorial talks, held Sept. 6, Wang announced that his government had approved the departure of 12 of 41 U.S. civilians detained in mainland China. Wang said that 9 of the 12 Americans concerned had applied for exit visas and could leave at once and that the 3 others would be granted visas when they applied.

The U.S. State Department called the Chinese announcement "encouraging" but said that the "piecemeal" release of Americans would not lessen the U.S. insistence that all 41 U.S. civilians be released before the Geneva talks passed to the "other practical matters" of the 2d point on the agenda.

Johnson and Wang reached Sept. 10 an accord on the repatriation of civilians. Their joint communiqué, issued the same date, stated that Communist China "recognizes that Americans. . .who desire to return to the U.S. are entitled to do so"; if any American believed he was "encountering obstruction in departure," he could inform the British chargé d'affaires in Peking and, "if desired by the U.S.," the British government "may also investigate the facts in any such case." For its part, the U.S. recognized that Chinese in the U.S. who wished to go to mainland China were "entitled to do so" and said that it would act "expeditiously" to further their departure. The Indian government was to be asked to help in the return of those Chinese by performing the same services for any Chinese "encountering obstruction" as the British would perform for the U.S. in China.

Wang told Johnson Sept. 10 that "within a few days" Peking would release 10 more U.S. civilians and that they would be sent to Hong Kong. This would bring the number of U.S. civilians released to a total of 22 out of 41 on the Chinese Communist list. Wang said others would be released "expeditiously." Peking radio said Sept. 11 that the 10 Americans had been convicted of crimes ranging from propagandizing to espionage but that their prison conduct was "fairly good" and that the 10, therefore, would be released "in advance of the expiration of their terms."

9 of the 10 Americans crossed into Hong Kong by Sept. 20. They were: the Rev. Harold W. Rigney of Chicago and Walter A. Rickett of Seattle, the latter a Fulbright student (Sept. 16); Lawrence Robert Buol of Stockton, Calif., a Nationalist China Civil Airlines employe (Sept. 17); American Dominican priests James G. Joyce of Clinton, Mass., Frederick A. Gordon of Somerset, Ohio and Joseph E. Hyde of Lowell, Mass. (Sept. 18); Rev. Levi A. Lovegren of Cherry Grove, Ore., Sarah Perkins of Charleston, S.C., a missionary-nurse, and Dorothy Middleton of Cicero, Ill., an inter-denominational missionary (Sept. 20). Rickett, 34, whose wife had been released from China in February, said in Hong Kong after his release: "I was engaged in espionage work. . . . I was an agent for the U.S. government. I collected military information. . . , and I was guilty." He said that the Communists had treated him leniently and that he was convinced the U.S. had used bacteriological warfare in Korea.

The Chinese Communist Party organ *Jenmin Jih Pao* (*People's Daily*) had said Sept. 12 that the agreement on the release of civilians was "a good beginning" and "creates an atmosphere of mutual confidence between China and the U.S." The newspaper expressed hope for "further negotiations."

Talks Reach Impasse

Once the agreement on civilian repatriation had been arrived at, Communist China sought to move the ambassadorial talks to the next item on the agenda ("other practical matters"). Wang Sept. 14 proposed "high-level" U.S.-Communist Chinese talks. Johnson replied that "it would be premature to discuss other matters" before the Americans actually had been released. At the meeting of Sept. 20, however, Johnson agreed to move to the next item on the agenda, keeping open the question of civilian repatriation for further discussion.

Soon afterwards, the ambassadorial talks reached an impasse. State Secy. Dulles said at his news conference Dec. 6, 1955 that the Geneva talks "are not making as good progress as could be hoped." Dulles criticized "the lack of actual action under the agreement already reached" on the release of U.S. citizens in mainland China. "There has been a measure of compliance with that, but not yet a full measure," he said. Dulles observed that the talks were "proceeding in a normal way, having regard to the character of the people we are talking with."

The U.S. State Department protested Dec. 16, 1955 against the continued detention of U.S. civilians in China in view of the Sept. 1955 agreement on the return of civilians in both countries. "All U.S. citizens should have been out of Communist China long before this," the State Department statement said. The Communist Chinese Consulate in Geneva had contended Dec. 15 that Peking had "faithfully" carried out the agreement on civilians but that the U.S. had violated the "letter and spirit" of the accord. The State Department replied Dec. 16 that "not a single Chinese has been refused exit" from the U.S., and that the Indian embassy, which was to act as representative for Communist China on the question of detained civilians, had not approached the U.S. on the subject.

The U.S. Immigration Service announced Jan. 5, 1956 that Liu Yung-ming, a patient in the State Mental Hospital in Farmington, Mo., was able to travel alone. He was discharged and began his return to China Jan. 7. Peking had protested that Liu was being held in the U.S. against his will. Liu had been in the hospital since 1949 and had been subject to deportation since 1951 as a public charge.

The Communist Chinese Foreign Ministry charged that 2 U.S. military planes had "intruded" over Manchuria Jan. 10, creating "a grave act of military provocation." It reported that Chinese planes "took off immediately in pursuit and the American military planes fled." The incident "shows that the U.S. is sparing no effort in its attempt to create tension in the Far East," Peking radio quoted the ministry spokesman as saying. The Peking official added that "no foreign interference will be allowed" in the freeing of U.S. civilians still in mainland China. He said that Americans who "offended against the law in China must be dealt with in accordance with Chinese legal procedures, and no time limit can be set for their release."

U.S. State Department officials said that they knew nothing of the incident.

Dulles' 'Brink of War' Thesis

A new issue arose from a "brink of war" thesis attributed to U.S. State Secy. Dulles. In the Jan. 16, 1956 issue of *Life* magazine (published Jan. 11), Time-Life Washington Bureau Chief James Shepley quoted Dulles as saying:

● "It is a pretty fair inference" that the Eisenhower Administration's "policy of deterrance," under which the Chinese Communists were made to know that new aggression would provoke strong U.S. retaliation, had "brought the Korean war to an end . . . , kept the Chinese from sending their Red armies into Indochina" and "stopped them in Formosa."

● "We were brought to the verge of war" in taking strong action on the risk that it would maintain peace, but "the ability to get to the verge without getting into the war is the necessary art. If you cannot master it, you inevitably get into war. If you try to run away from it, if you are scared to go to the brink, you are lost. We've had to look it square in the face—on the question of enlarging the Korean War, on the question of getting into the Indochina war, on the question of Formosa. We walked to the brink and we looked it in the face. We took strong action. It took a lot more courage for the President than for me. His was the ultimate decision. . . ."

Shepley said in his article (entitled *How Dulles Averted War*) that these actions were taken in the Korean, Indochinese and Taiwan Straits crises (quotations from Shepley):

Korea—Pres. Eisenhower, returning from his pre-inauguration visit to Korea in November and December 1952, agreed with Dulles that great wars started because aggressors thought they could get by with aggression. Eisenhower decided that he would make every effort to reach an honorable Korean truce with the Communists but, if truce efforts failed, would "fight to win"—attacking Communist bases in Manchuria and employing a "tactical use of atomic arms."

Dulles, during an official visit to India in May 1953, had told Indian Prime Min. Jawaharlal Nehru of the decision in the belief that Nehru would impress its meaning on Communist Chinese leaders. "Within 2 weeks" Communist truce negotiators in Korea had "begun to negotiate seriously." The Communists later abstained from renewing the war when Pres. Syngman Rhee of South Korea tried to goad them into it by releasing prisoners of war held in South Korea.

Formosa—War was "avoided mainly by" the Dulles-authored U.S. Congressional resolution (the "Formosa Resolution") passed in Jan. 1955, authorizing the President to use U.S. forces to repel a Communist attack on Taiwan; Dulles gave a 2d warning via Burmese Prime Min. U Nu that the U.S. "meant business" about Taiwan; Dulles "never doubted" that the President would regard a Communist attack on Quemoy and Matsu as menacing Taiwan.

Indochina—Dulles and Adm. Arthur Radford, Joint

Chiefs of Staff chairman, had obtained Eisenhower's approval in Apr. 1954 for the use of U.S. air power to destroy Communist staging bases in China if the mainland Chinese "intervened openly" in Indochina. 2 U.S. aircraft carriers (the *Boxer* and the *Philippine Sea*) bearing atomic weapons were sent to the South China Sea while Dulles sought and "thought he had" agreements with Britain and France on joint intervention in Indochina if necessary. Britain then underwent a "change of heart," and France's government of Pierre Mendès-France "evidently wanted to dump the load" of the Indochina war "at any cost." But "Dulles had seen to it that [Communist China and the USSR] knew that the U.S. was prepared to act decisively to prevent the fall of all of southeast Asia," so the French and British were "able to bargain from Dulles' strength" at the mid-1954 Geneva conference and save all but northern Vietnam.

The publication of the Shepley article drew sharp criticism from the Democrats. Sen. Hubert H. Humphrey (Minn.) launched a series of Democratic attacks on the "brink of war" statement when he said in the Senate Jan. 12, 1956 that Dulles' "fraudulent reassertion" of the policy of "massive retaliation" would cause "untold trouble with our allies." Humphrey said Jan. 13 that "Mr. Dulles' 'art'. . . comes precariously close to rejecting the traditional American conviction that we must not strike the first blow [nor] bear the awful responsibility for beginning atomic war." The Senator demanded that Eisenhower say whether he agreed with Dulles.

Adlai E. Stevenson said in Chicago Jan. 14 that he was "shocked that the Secretary of State is willing to play Russian roulette with the life of our nation. . . . The art of diplomacy, especially in this atomic age, must lead to peace, not war or the brink of war."

Leading British newspapers denied Jan. 13 that the British government in indorsing Southeast Asian collective defense in Apr. 1954, had committed itself to intervene in the Indochinese war. U.S. press reports from Paris Jan. 14 said that Frenchmen doubted that Communist China had ever intended to enter the Indochina war or that Dulles' moves had a major effect on Indochina armistice terms. Moscow's *Izvestia* denounced Dulles Jan. 14 for the "encouragement of bellicose statements by American generals and admirals."

Rallying to Dulles' support, Republican Reps. Stephen B. Derounian and Harold C. Ostertag (N.Y.), Patrick J. Hillings and Joseph F. Holt (Calif.), Joseph P. O'Hara (Minn.), John J. Rhodes (Ariz.) and John M. Robsion Jr. (Ky.) issued a statement in Washington Jan. 14. The statement praised Dulles for his renunciation of the "old Truman-Acheson policy of appeasement and surrender to the Communists."

Vice Pres. Richard M. Nixon said in Springfield, Ill. Jan. 14 that "the test of a foreign policy is its ability to keep the peace without surrendering any territory or principle," and "that great fact about the Eisenhower-Dulles foreign policy will stand out long after the tempest in a teapot over the expression ['brink of war'] is forgotten." Nixon also declared Jan. 15 that Stevenson, in describing Dulles' methods as "Russian roulette," used "destructive terminology" to describe "honest and sincere decisions. . . ."

Dulles himself came to the defense of the statement attributed to him. In his news conference Jan. 17, he verified the "substance" of quotations "specifically attributed to me" by Shepley but refused to discuss other parts of the article. Dulles asserted his belief that "the surest way to avoid war is to let it be known in advance that we are prepared to defend" basic moral values and vital interests. He said that the U.S. was "brought to the verge of war" because of Communist threats against Korea, Indochina and Taiwan.

Peking & Washington Disclose Talks Secrets

In the heated atmosphere in the U.S. over the Dulles' "brink of war" diplomacy, the proceedings of the Geneva ambassadorial talks came to light, unexpectedly, by public announcement first by Peking Jan. 18, 1956 and then by the U.S. State Department Jan. 21.

The Communist Chinese Foreign Ministry said in Peking: It was issuing its report on the talks because "the U.S. has recently stepped up military activities in the Taiwan area to aggravate the tension, and U.S. Secy. of State Dulles even renewed the clamors for an atomic war against China." Dulles had "openly cried out recently that in order to hold on to China's territory and infringe China's sovereignty, he would not scruple to start an atomic war."

The U.S. State Department said Jan. 21 that the Chinese had "issued a misleading statement" on the Geneva talks and that it was "necessary that the record be set straight" through an American statement in reply.

The Peking and Washington statements disclosed that the U.S. had proposed that the agreement on civilian repatriation in Sept. 1955 be followed by a statement renouncing the use of force by Communist China and the U.S. The 2 accounts of the talks showed that Communist China refused to apply such a declaration to the "internal affair" of Taiwan and that the U.S. had charged the Communist Chinese with trying to exempt from the declaration areas they meant to seize by force.

Otherwise, the 2 statements differed in particulars. The following is the chronological summary and conflicting explanations:

(1) Peking said: It first had proposed a discussion of the trade embargo against Communist China and the possibility of "negotiations at a higher level" to settle Sino-American disputes; Communist China had "advocated consistently" the peaceful settlement of Sino-U.S. disputes "in accordance

with the purposes and principles of the UN Charter" and, therefore, had suggested Sino-U.S. negotiations during the Bandung Conference in Apr. 1955; the U.S. had rejected "any substantive discussion" of the trade embargo and Communist China's bid for higher-level talks when Johnson and Wang met; then the U.S. Oct. 8 "suggested. . .a declaration on the renunciation of the use of force."

The U.S. statement asserted that Johnson had pointed out that "continuing Communist threats to Taiwan" obstructed progress toward a Sino-U.S. settlement and had suggested a mutual renunciation of force "generally, and particularly in the Taiwan area" to permit peaceful negotiations.

(2) Peking said: Wang Oct. 27, 1955 had introduced a draft renouncing the use of force. But it was rejected by Johnson because of U.S. "unwillingness" to have particular stipulations of the UN charter specifically mentioned (or) to have the announcement explicitly provide for "a meeting of U.S. and Communist Chinese foreign ministers.

The U.S. said: Communist China's Oct. 27 draft was unacceptable because it "pointedly omitted any reference to the Taiwan area" or "recognition of the right of self-defense"; the Communists might hold that such a document "did not apply to the Taiwan area, which is the very place against which the Communist threats are directed," and cite it as evidence that "the U.S. had renounced the right to use force in self-defense."

According to the U.S. State Department version, Johnson Nov. 10 had introduced an alternate draft saying that the renunciation of force would be "without prejudice to the peaceful pursuit of its policies by either side [and] did not deprive either side of the right of self-defense."

Peking denounced these U.S. specifications as an "attempt to confuse the international dispute between China and the U.S. in the Taiwan area with the domestic matter between the Chinese government and the Chiang Kai-shek clique" and to force Communist China to "accept...U.S. occupation of China's territory, Taiwan, and give up its sovereign right to liberate Taiwan." Peking said: Communist China "has repeatedly declared that it would strive for the liberation of Taiwan by peaceful means so far as it is possible. But this internal affair of China's cannot possibly be a subject of the Sino-American talks."

(3) The U.S. account of the Geneva talks said that a 2d Chinese proposal made Dec. 1 had been "an advance" in that it had "dropped the provision for talks on the foreign minister level in favor of the continuance of ambassadorial talks, but still pointedly omitted any references to the Taiwan area and to recognition of the right of self-defense." The U.S. said that Johnson had "suggested 2 simple amendments to the Communist counter-proposal" Jan. 12: "insertion of the words 'without prejudice to the inherent right of individual and collective self-defense' and of the words 'in the Taiwan area or elsewhere.'"

(4) Peking's statement Jan. 18 said that the U.S. had "no reason whatsoever to continue to drag out the talks" if it "really has the sincerity to renounce the use or threat of force." Peking added that "the only practical and feasible means for settling disputes between China and the U.S., particularly a serious question such as the tension in the Taiwan area," was a Sino-U.S. foreign ministers' conference.

Referring to the 1955 agreement on civilians, Peking said that the U.S. "kept raising groundless charges" about Chinese detention of U.S. civilians, while "the great majority" of "tens of thousands of Chinese in the U.S." had "not been able or not dared to apply for returning to China" because of U.S. "obstructions and threats...in violation of the agreement."

The U.S. statement Jan. 21 said "13 Americans are still held in Communist prisons" 4 months after Peking promised their release. The U.S. demanded "the now overdue fulfillment" of that agreement, "not only for humanitarian reasons but because respect for international undertakings lies at the foundation of a stable international order."

(5) The U.S. statement made specific reference to the following passage in the Peking statement of Jan. 18: "Taiwan is China's territory. There can be no question of defense, so far as the U.S. is concerned. The U.S. has already used force and the threat of force against China in the Taiwan area.... Yet the U.S. has demanded the right of defense in the Taiwan area. Is this not precisely a demand that China accept continued U.S. occupation of Taiwan and that the tension in the Taiwan area be maintained forever?"

From this the State Department drew the conclusion that "the Communists so far seem willing to renounce force only if they are first conceded the goals for which they would use force."

The Communist Chinese Foreign Ministry said Jan. 24 that the U.S. would be responsible for "all the consequences" if the Geneva talks broke down on the problems of Taiwan and civilian repatriation. In Geneva, Communist Chinese Amb. Wang Ping-nan said that the U.S. was prolonging the talks as part of a "brink-of-war policy."

U.S. State Secy. Dulles said at his news conference Jan. 24 that the U.S. statement of Jan. 21 indicated to him that "some progress has been made" at Geneva. "Negotiations with the Chinese Communists are usually slow and pro-longed," but "we are planning to go ahead.... and we con-tinue to be patient and persistent in our effort to obtain a greater assurance of peace and renunciation of force in that area," Dulles said.

Geneva Talks Drift

The ambassadorial talks were continued without produc-ing any new agreement. A State Department communiqué of June 12, 1956 stated that Amb. U. Alexis Johnson had presented to Amb. Wang Ping-nan Apr. 19 a U.S. proposal

for the renunciation of force "in the Taiwan area or elsewhere." According to the State Department, the proposal
was "identical to the Communist proposal of Dec. 1, 1955"
but Wang had rejected it on grounds that it had condoned
U.S. "interference in China's internal affairs and its occupation of Taiwan." The State Department rejected the Communist Chinese proposal for talks between State Secy.
Dulles and Premier-Foreign Minister Chou En-lai.

Wang had revealed in Geneva earlier June 12 that he
had asked the U.S. May 12 to agree to a foreign ministers'
meeting within 2 months and to issue a joint declaration with
Communist China of the 2 nations' intentions to settle the
Taiwan dispute through peaceful negotiations.

With the Geneva talks apparently stalemated, Chou
En-lai stressed a "peaceful liberation of Taiwan." In an
interview with a Reuters correspondent June 1, Chou said
the prospect for "peaceful liberation of Taiwan is becoming
brighter every day." He said that his government would not
let the U.S. use the Geneva talks to "legitimize U.S. occupation of Taiwan" by suggesting that both sides issue a joint
statement guaranteeing the *status quo* of the island. He said
his government would agree to a "joint statement that the
2 countries are willing to use peaceful means to settle the
dispute. . .including talks at a foreign ministers' level."

Speaking before the National People's Congress June 28,
Chou formally declared that his government was "willing
to discuss with the Taiwan authorities specific steps for the
peaceful liberation of Taiwan." He reiterated Communist
claims on the island. A Nationalist government statement in
Taipei June 29 denounced Chou's offer as "insulting" and
said: "What needs liberating now is. . .the mainland under
the bloody Communist reign." Chou predicted in his June
28 speech that "traditional friendships" of the Chinese and
American people eventually would lead to diplomatic recognition of his government by the U.S.

U.S. POLICY TESTED (1956-7)

Policy Changes in Peking

The uneasy situation in Communist China and throughout the Communist world in 1956 and 1957 seemed to establish the likelihood of a more accommodating Communist Chinese attitude toward the U.S. Peking made a prolonged effort—from mid-1956 to the spring of 1957—to induce Washington to recognize the Communists as China's legitimate rulers.

The monolithic façade of the Communist world cracked wide open in 1956 and fissures appeared within the Soviet domestic structure as well as in eastern Europe. Matters seem to have started when Nikita S. Khrushchev, first secretary of the Soviet Communist Party, delivering a speech Feb. 24–5 before a closed session of the 20th Soviet Party Congress, bitterly criticized the late Joseph V. Stalin. Not until late in June 1957, when Khrushchev ousted his 3 chief rivals from the party leadership, did the situation in the Kremlin return to relative calm.

By then, China had entered a period of flux. Chinese Communist Party Chairman Mao Tse-tung had also initiated a brief—but turbulent—era of intellectual freedom with his "100 Flowers" speech: "Let 100 flowers blossom" and "Let 100 schools of thought contend." This speech was delivered in Peking May 2, 1956 at a closed session of the Supreme State Conference, an advisory arm of the Chinese Communist government. In a speech before same body in Peking Feb. 27, 1957, Mao reportedly admitted that his régime had "liquidated" 800,000 Chinese in the period from Oct. 1949 to early 1954 but said that further terror would be counterproductive.

The subsequent relatively liberal months in China produced so much criticism of Mao and his régime, however, that official tolerance of verbal expressions of dissent abruptly ended by mid-1957 and a period of harsh reaction set in.

Peking's Drive for U.S. Recognition

Chinese Premier Chou En-lai continued on the diplomatic front Peking's political offensive against the U.S. policy of nonrecognition. His technique was alternately to soften and stiffen his tone on the themes of civility and sovereignty.

In an interview granted Australian newsman Reg B. Leonard, Chou said Aug. 5, 1956 that China could soon "enlarge the democratic base of our system of government" through more frequent meetings of the National People's Congress, greater use of criticism and the extension of voting privileges to ex-landlords and to confessed ex-counter-revolutionaries. Then, criticizing the U.S. refusal to recognize the Peking government, Chou rejected any U.S. participation in any negotiations on the future of Taiwan. He asserted that the island was a Chinese province and that how it should be "liberated" was a matter of Chinese sovereignty.

The Peking government Aug. 6 cabled offers of visas to 15 U.S. newsmen who had requested them. They were invited to China for a month-long visit to begin Aug. 20–30. Lincoln White, U.S. State Department press officer, said Aug. 6 that the U.S. would continue to bar travel in Communist China on U.S. passports under criminal statute penalties of a $2,000 fine and up to 5 years in jail. The State Department Aug. 7 acknowledged the receipt of newsmen's protests but said that the ban would remain as long as U.S. citizens were held in China as "political hostages."

Chou continued to sound a conciliatory note toward the U.S. He went to New Delhi Nov. 28 on an extended tour of 7 Asian countries, addressed the Indian parliament Nov. 29 and conferred with Indian Prime Min. Jawaharlal Nehru.

According to Nehru, who spoke with American correspondents Dec. 12 during his Washington trip, Chou's "attitude seemed to be one of desiring to have much better relations" with the U. S. This desire, Nehru observed, seemed "definitely" stronger than the attitude he had seen during Chou's previous visit to India 2½ years previously.

Chou had hinted before leaving New Delhi Dec. 1 that Americans jailed in Communist China might be freed for good behavior before their sentences were completed. He suggested in Calcutta Dec. 9 that the U.S. should make the next move if it wanted American prisoners in China freed and if it desired a Far Eastern settlement. He repeated the charge, repeatedly denied by U.S. officials, that Chinese who wanted to return to China were kept in U.S. jails.

In Katmandu, Nepal, Chou intimated Jan. 29, 1957— for the 3d time in 2 months—that Peking might release another group of 10 U.S. prisoners for good behavior before they completed their jail terms. He said that his government wanted to be friends with the U.S., and he again offered to meet with State Secy. John Foster Dulles, but he complained that "even when we extend our hand, they refuse to shake hands with us."

In Mar. 1957, Chou repeated his call for negotiations with the U.S. In a speech before the Political Consultative Conference in Peking Mar. 5, Chou charged the U.S. with refusal "to negotiate seriously on the question of tension in the Taiwan area" and with "planning to install guided missiles" on Taiwan to make it into an American "dependency, like Hawaii." Chou accused the U.S. of instigating a "so-called free China" group "to overthrow the Taiwan authorities." He reiterated the Communists' intent to "liberate" Taiwan peacefully.

Red Chinese Unrest Hardens U.S. Attitude

Meanwhile, the sudden reversal of the Soviet Communist Party policy had produced severe repercussions in the

Soviet bloc. An uprising took place in Poznan, Poland, in June 1956. This was followed late in October by an even bloodier revolt in Hungary. From China there was a report of revolt in Szechuan; Chou En-lai confirmed the report Dec. 9. The revolt, said Chou, had been caused "by a lack of understanding. . . of the policy of the Chinese government." But he said that "this is settled" and that "Chinese armed forces" had quelled the outbreak.

These developments in the Communist world were seen in the U.S. State Department as attesting to the wisdom of the U.S. policy toward Communist China. State Secy. Dulles addressing the South-East Asia Treaty Organization (SEATO) Council in Bangkok, Thailand Mar. 11, 1957, observed that events had proved communism to be "a passing and not a permanent phase" for Asia. He said Mar. 12 that the U.S. "adheres steadfastly" to its recognition of the Nationalist Chinese government on Taiwan. He held that U.S. recognition or UN membership for Communist China "would serve no national purpose" but instead would "encourage influences hostile to us and to our allies."

Dulles repeated these views June 28, 1957 in a speech at a convention of the Lions International in San Francisco. In what was called by the State Department a "major" foreign policy pronouncement, Dulles said that "it would be folly" for the U.S. to make diplomatic, commercial or cultural concessions to Communist China and thus "enhance" any Communist ability to harm the U.S. and its allies. He said the U.S. would fight Communist China's entry into the UN, where, as a "veto-wielding member of the Security Council," Peking could "implant in the [UN] the seeds of its own [the UN's] destruction." Dulles conceded that U.S. policy toward Communist China, "like all our policies," was under "periodic review." However, he continued, "the Chinese people are, above all, individualistic. . . . We can confidently base our policies on the assumption that international communism's rule of strict conformity is, in China as elsewhere, a passing and not a perpetual phase. We owe it to ourselves, our allies and the Chinese people to do all that we can to contribute to that passing."

In remarks presumably directed at U.S. allies seeking to increase trade and normalize relations with mainland China, Dulles warned that such actions would only "build up the military power of the [U.S.'] potential enemy." He rejected theories to the effect that "if we assist the Chinese Communists to wax strong, they will inevitably break with Soviet Russia." Diplomatic recognition of the Peking régime, he said, would (1) "immensely" discourage mainland Chinese from seeking a change in their government, (2) cause "millions of overseas Chinese in free Asian countries" to accept Communist Chinese leadership, (3) break U.S. treaty pledges to the Nationalist Chinese government and (4) "gravely" perplex other free Asians.

Thus, American leaders confirmed, the U.S. was firmly fixed in its policy of nonrecognition of Communist China. In line with this policy, the State Department consistently refused to be drawn into discussion with Communist China on political matters that might lead to normalization of diplomatic relations with Peking. Moreover, the State Department imposed a ban on trade with Communist China by U.S. citizens and on travel to Communist China by American newsmen. The U.S. also sought to maintain a trade embargo against mainland China by other North Atlantic Treaty Organization (NATO) powers and Japan consistent with a resolution adopted by the UN during the Korean War. This U.S. policy caused dissension in allied councils.

U.S. Fights Pressure for Trade with Peking

The U.S. Commerce Department Mar. 28, 1957 revoked the export license rights of a British bank, the Anglo-Continental Exchange, Ltd., and 4 foreign firms controlled by financier William Wallersteiner, because of the shipment of $46,000 worth of U.S.-produced aureomycin to mainland China via Poland in 1954.

Under mounting pressure from European nations, however, the U.S. Government reviewed its policy on trade with Communist China. Commerce Secy. Sinclair Weeks said Apr. 4 that the U.S. would agree to relax Communist Chinese trade controls if other Western nations accepted tighter restrictions on trade with the USSR and Soviet-bloc nations.

Pres. Eisenhower conceded to newsmen Apr. 10 that "there has been a constant flow of staff work" on "bringing more closely together the forbidden [trade] lists for [the] Soviets and for China." The President noted the foreign trade problems of Britain and Japan and said that "if we are going to keep Japan our friends," the U.S. cannot tell the Japanese government: "Now, you mustn't trade with... the great area right next to you...which has been your traditional trading area." He emphasized that there was little "prospect of keeping Japan a viable economy merely by giving them some cash each year."

Ian Harvey, British joint parliamentary Foreign Affairs undersecretary, told the British House of Commons Apr. 18 that Britain would act in its own "economic interests" to bring "into line" varying restrictions on trade with Communist China and the USSR. Harvey said that the U.S. had been informed of the British position "in no uncertain terms" during recent Bermuda talks between Eisenhower and Prime Min. Harold Macmillan. (Reports Apr. 22 valued January-February 1957 British imports from mainland China at $8.4 million, British exports to Communist China during the same period at $5.1 million.)

The U.S. State Department announced Apr. 20 that it was "prepared to discuss certain modifications in the existing system" of "multilateral controls on trade with Communist China." The announcement said that the U.S. had proposed a review of the trade policies "in an effort to meet the views of its allies" and "continue to maintain effective multilateral controls" on Western trade with mainland China. It "emphasized" that the U.S. "will continue its unilateral embargo on all trade with Communist China." The announcement said that the U.S., in notes to 14 countries cooperating in the Communist-China trade controls, had proposed that: (1) "certain items for peaceful use which now are embargoed" "would be removed from controls and...placed on the same basis as in the case of trade with the East European Soviet bloc"; (2) "other items...would continue under embargo and would be transferred to the east European Soviet-bloc list but under a lesser degree of control"; (3) the "exceptions procedure" on embargoed goods would be tightened.

The NATO powers established a special committee (NATO Chincom) to discuss, with a view toward strategic control, the trade with Communist China. The committee met in Paris in May. Several European countries rejected U.S. arguments for curbing trade with mainland China more stringently than with Russia. The British were said to have contended that (1) Communist China, indirectly, was already getting items denied it but sold to other Communist states, and (2) China's stockpiling of semistrategic items could be checked more effectively if the Communist Chinese were dealt with directly and their imports of Western goods supervised properly.

Following the discussion in the NATO Chincom, British Foreign Secy. Selwyn Lloyd disclosed in the House of Commons in London May 30 that Britain would modify its restrictions on exports to mainland China to make them correspond to those applied to exports to the USSR.

Under Britain's modified policy, both Communist China and the USSR were barred from buying munitions, atomic energy materials and supplies and about 200 other strategic items. About 200 other items, including industrial machinery, transportation equipment, rubber and numerous chemicals, became available to Communist China the same as to Russia. It was estimated that the new policy would result in British exports to mainland China valued at about £20 million ($56 million) a year as against the current £10 million ($28 million) rate.

The U.S. State Department let it be known May 30, 1957 that it was "most disappointed" by Britain's decision on trade with Communist China. Pres. Eisenhower said at his news conference June 5: "I don't see as much advantage in maintaining the differential [between restrictions on Soviet and Chinese trade] as some people do, although I have never advocated its complete elimination." The President said he felt that trade with mainland China "cannot be stopped" and would be "clandestine" if not "authorized." But he expressed the opinion that "the law" would curb the sale of some U.S. goods to China and said that the law would be enforced. (The 1951 Battle Act was regarded by Congressional legal experts as requiring the President to withhold weapons, oil and machinery of strategic importance from Communist China, a Korean War enemy. The Trading-with-the-Enemy and Export Control acts were regarded as leaving export controls to the President's discretion.)

Sen. William F. Knowland (R., Calif.), Senate minority leader, said May 31 that Britain's move to liberalize trade with Communist China "can only strengthen our common enemies both in Asia and in Europe." Sen. Lyndon B. Johnson (D., Tex.), Senate majority leader, said June 1 that "the British action will require us to reevaluate the Chinese trade situation" and that "that new look will be one of our most pressing foreign-policy problems" in 1957. Sen. Allen J. Ellender (D., La.) said on ABC-TV's "Celebrity Parade" program June 2 that the U.S. "might look into the feasibility of selling some of our nonstrategic materials" to Communist China.

State Secy. Dulles said at a news conference June 11 that Eisenhower, the State Department and a majority of the U.S.' allies in NATO Chincom wished to maintain more rigid controls on trade with Communist China than on trade with eastern Europe. Referring to Eisenhower's indication that he apparently no longer favored a total ban on trade with mainland China, Dulles noted that the President had backed a continuation of the "China differential" for the time being. Alluding to Britain's decision to modify its controls on trade with Communist China, Dulles said that "the views of the ... [U.S.], which carries the primary responsibility for peace in the area, should have weight with respect to that matter."

Sen. Warren G. Magnuson (D., Wash.), Senate Commerce Committee chairman, urged June 16 that U.S. airlines be permitted to fly passengers and mail to Communist China as a possible preliminary step toward relaxing U.S.-Chinese trade barriers. (The Belgian and Netherlands governments had announced June 14 their decision to relax controls on mainland Chinese trade to conform with restrictions against commerce with the USSR. West Germany announced a similar decision June 18.)

U.S. Press Questions Travel Ban

The State Department ran into difficulties at home with the press over the restriction it was imposing on American newsmen who wanted to travel in Communist China. State Secy. Dulles, at his news conference Feb. 6, 1957, denied that the restriction was being imposed in order to withhold information from the U.S. public. Dulles said that China had been "trying to get reporters—preferably those it picked—to come," and had "tried to use the illegal detention of Americans" in China to force State Department approval of the trips. The U.S., he said, could not permit other governments to "throw into jail American citizens, so they can put a price on their release." He added that "the issuance of passports to a régime which is not recognized is something which is never done."

Much of the U.S. press questioned the State Department's policy, but the management of at least one radio network did not do so openly—and censored those of its editorial staff who did. Sen. A. S. (Mike) Monroney (D., Okla.) charged Feb. 11 that CBS had prevented radio newscaster Eric Sevareid from commenting Feb. 6 on the China travel ban. CBS News Director John Day said Feb. 11 that Sevareid's script had violated CBS rules in that it was editorial rather than analytical. (Edward R. Murrow was reported Feb. 12 to have been rebuked by CBS officials for a commentary on the China travel ban aired on CBS radio Feb. 6.) Pres. William Dwight of the American Newspaper Publishers Association protested to the State Department Feb. 6 against the travel ban.

William Worthy Jr., 35, a U.S. newsman who had visited mainland China in defiance of the State Department ban, returned to the U.S. Feb. 10 via Moscow and Budapest, where he had refused U.S. diplomats' demands Feb. 7 that he yield his passport. Worthy said that he had "challenged the government" and was "prepared to take all the consequences." *Look* magazine writer Edmund Stevens and photographer Philip Harrington left China for Moscow Jan. 21. Harrington returned to the U.S. without incident Jan. 29. Stevens remained in Moscow, where he was told that his passport would be invalidated for all travel except back to the U.S. Gardner Cowles, the magazine's president and editor, said Feb. 10 that he would ask for an open State Department hearing on the Stevens and Harrington passport cases.

State Secy. Dulles said at a news conference Mar. 5 that the U.S. was seeking a way to reverse the ban on newsmen's travel to Communist China "to satisfy better the demand for news coverage without seeming to drop the barriers down generally." He said that travel to mainland China by U.S. reporters "would be bearable by us" but might have "dangerous consequences in other areas." He then disclosed that the State Department had no plans to take legal action against the 3 U.S. newsmen who had defied the ban.

Pres. Eisenhower said at his press conference Mar. 7 that the U.S. had "studied this very earnestly to see how we could secure from China more news without appearing to be accepting Red China on the same cultural basis that we do...other nations." "I can't offer at the moment any change in policy."

Testifying before the Senate Foreign Relations Committee Apr. 2, Deputy State Undersecy. Robert Murphy said that the U.S. would not yield to Communist Chinese "blackmail" and let U.S. newsmen go to China until 8 Americans still held by the Peking government were released. Murphy confirmed Apr. 2 that the State Department had "tentatively declined" Apr. 1 to renew William Worthy's passport. He denied exerting "pressure" on CBS Chairman William S. Paley to suppress films taken by Worthy in China.

The board of directors of the Associated Press, in its annual report issued Apr. 23, cited the lack of reliable news on China as "the most noticeable gap in...[AP's] coverage" and said that "it believes qualified newsmen should be allowed to report first-hand from the mainland of China."

State Secy. Dulles invited "the newsgathering community" Apr. 23 to propose plans under which "a strictly limited number of responsible correspondents" could "go to Communist China on behalf of that newsgathering community as a whole." Dulles offered a controlled relaxation of the State Department ban on travel to mainland China by U.S. newsmen to "permit responsible news gathering and at the same time not permit a general influx of Americans into Communist China."

Dulles said that the State Department "would be glad to have the American public get information about Communist China first-hand through [U.S.] correspondents." "On the other hand," he added, "we are not willing to permit Americans generally to go into ... [Communist China], where the Trading-with-the-Enemy Act still applies and where Americans" have been held "as political hostages." Dulles asserted that "a selective experiment" involving a trip to Communist China by a small number of newsmen "could be made, consistent with our general policy."

Intellectual Dissent Reported in China

Signs of serious domestic unrest within Communist China came to public notice in the U.S. in June 1957. The *N.Y. Times* June 10 published a version of Mao Tse-tung's secret speech before the closed session of the Advisory Supreme State Conference Feb. 27, 1957. The Hsinhua (New China) News Agency provided its own version June 18.

Hsinhua's version of the speech, entitled "The Correct Handling of Contradictions Among the People," admittedly was edited by the Peking government, apparently to remove any pointed criticism of Soviet policies and admission of Chinese mistakes—passages that had appeared in earlier versions and of which knowledge had been obtained in the West.

According to a version of the address reported June 12 by Sidney Gruson, *N.Y. Times* Warsaw correspondent, Mao had conceded that: (a) 800,000 Chinese had been "liquidated" by Communist security forces between Oct. 1949 and early 1954; (b) problems of conflict within Communist society "are new in Marxism-Leninism" and were viewed "negatively" by Stalin, who instituted "a rule of terror and the liquidation of thousands of Communists"; (c) the continued use of terror would result in situations similar to "the

tragedy of Hungary," where the Communist Party disap-
peared in a "few days" and the state threatened to disintegrate.

In this speech, Mao made these ideological comments
on the following topics:

Contradictions—"It would be naive to imagine that there are no more
contradictions" in Chinese society between "the government and the masses."
But these contradictions, "if properly handled, can be transformed into a
nonantagonistic" pattern and "resolved in a peaceful way." "Ours is a
people's democratic dictatorship, led by the working class and based on the
worker-peasant alliance." The régime's "first function is to suppress the
reactionary classes...and those exploiters in the country who range themselves against the Socialist revolution."

"Certain people in our country were delighted when the Hungarian
events took place. They hoped that something similar would happen in
China." But "such hopes ran counter to the interests of the masses and
therefore could not possibly get their support."

Others hoped "for the adoption of the 2-party system of the West,
where one party is in office and the other out of office. But this so-called
2-party system is nothing but a means of maintaining the dictatorship of the
bourgeoisie," and "where there is democracy for the bourgeoisie there can
be no democracy for the proletariat."

"While we stand for freedom with leadership and democracy under
centralized guidance, in no sense do we mean that coercive measures should
be taken to settle ideological matters and questions involving the distinction
between right and wrong among the people." "We cannot abolish religion
by administrative orders; nor can we force people not to believe in it. We
cannot compel people to give up idealism, any more than we can force them
to believe in Marxism." A "Socialist society grows more united and con-
solidated precisely through the ceaseless process of correctly dealing with
and resolving contradictions."

Agriculture, industry, intellectuals & minorities—Contradictions continued to exist "between the state and the cooperatives" (collective farms) and
"within and among the cooperatives themselves." 70% of the 500 million
Chinese peasants, however, actively supported the cooperative movement.
China's food crops had increased from 105 million tons in 1949 to more than
180 million tons in 1956. Under China's joint state-private ownership system,
contradictions continued to exist between workers and the former owners
who were currently used as managers. "Most" former businessmen "are
being transformed from exploiters into working people living by their own
labor."

"Several million intellectuals who worked for the old society have come
to serve the new society"; many had expressed themselves "in favor of the
Socialist system." "We should not be too exacting in what we expect of them.
As long as they comply with the requirements of the state and engage in
legitimate pursuits, we should give them opportunities for suitable work."

But "there has been a falling off in ideological and political work among students and intellectuals, and some unhealthy tendencies have appeared." "Not to have a correct political point of view is like having no soul."

China's minorities numbered 30 million but "inhabit regions which altogether comprise 50% to 60% of the country's total area." "The key to the solution of [the minority] question lies in overcoming Great-Han [Chinese] chauvinism" and "local nationalism." In "certain places" both problems "still exist in a serious degree, and this calls for our close attention." Although agreement had been reached on Tibetan reforms, "it has now been decided not to proceed with democratic reform in Tibet during the period of the 2d 5-year plan" but instead to implement it in the future "in the light of the situation obtaining at that time."

Criticism—Under the slogans "Let 100 Flowers Blossom" and "Let 100 Schools of Thought Contend," Mao urged Chinese Marxists to accept non-Marxist criticism. "Marxism has also developed through struggle," so scientific and artistic disputes "should not be settled in summary fashion." "As a scientific truth, Marxism fears no criticism. If it did, and could be defeated in argument, it would be worthless." "Plants raised in hothouses are not likely to be robust"; counterrevolutionary ideas should be silenced, but other non-Marxist ideas could be overcome "only by employing methods of discussion, criticism and reasoning."

(The edited text stated that an acceptance of "contending" ideological viewpoints had been proposed "in the light of the specific conditions existing in China, on the basis of the recognition that various kinds of contradictions still exist in a Socialist society and in response to the country's urgent need to speed up its economic and cultural development." The text made no generalization on the function of non-Marxist criticism in other Socialist societies.)

Strikes—"Small numbers of workers and students" and "members of a small number of agricultural cooperatives" had gone on strike and "created disturbances" in 1956 because of "the failure [of responsible authorities] to satisfy certain of their demands for material benefits." "It is nothing to get alarmed about if small numbers of people should create disturbances," Chinese leaders should strive to (a) "stamp out bureaucracy" and "deal with contradictions in a proper way" and (b) "make use of these disturbances as a special means of improving our work and educating the cadres and the masses" to reach "solutions to those questions which have been neglected in the past."

Intellectual dissent surfaced after Mao's speech. For example, in an open letter to the Chinese Communist Party's *Jenmin Jih Pao* (*People's Daily*), the first of its kind published by the paper, Prof. Ko Pei-chi of People's University asserted that "to kill Communists and to overthrow you cannot be called unpatriotic because you Communists are no longer of service to the people." Ko's denunciation, published May 31 and reported from Hong Kong June 22, warned that "even if the Communist Party is destroyed, China will not perish. This is because we will not become traitors even if there is no guidance of the Communist Party."

In an apparent effort to encourage and yet restrain the *Cheng Feng* (rectification) campaign begun by the government, *Jenmin Jih Pao* indicated June 23 that while many "extremists" had taken advantage of the campaign, all Chinese had a right to join in the criticism. Dr. Lo Lhung-chi, timber industry minister, and Chang Po-chun, communications minister, both pro-Communist "democrats," were reported June 19 to be under sharp attack from the satellite "democratic" parties in the Communist-led National Front for their open criticism of the régime.

The Peking régime appeared to have concluded that critics of the government had gone too far in responding to Mao's invitation to "let 100 flowers blossom" and "let 100 schools of thought contend." Premier Chou En-lai warned June 26 that Chinese non-Communists would be classified as "enemies of the people" if they persisted in criticising the Communist régime. Chou, addressing the opening session of the National People's Congress (the Communist Chinese parliament) in Peking, rejected the idea of direct elections and a multi-party system as "bourgeois tricks" and said that Chinese Communist Party leaders would "allow no wavering on the basic state system of our country." Chou said he hoped that critics of the government, "profiting by their own experience," would "repent and accept opportunities of remolding themselves."

Lu Ting-yi, head of the Communist Party Committee's Central propaganda department, warned in an address before the National People's Congress July 12 that "rightists" had disseminated "fantastic anti-Socialist views" in an effort to "seize leadership" and instigate a "counterrevolutionary dictatorship."

An editorial in *Jenmin Jih Pao* warned July 12 that rightist "demons can be wiped out only when they. . .come out of the cage." Identified by Hong Kong Communists as written by Mao, the editorial said rightists were "poisonous weeds" which must "be got rid of."

Mrs. Soong Ching-ling, widow of Sun Yat-sen, the founder of the Chinese Republic, called for the complete acceptance of the Communist Party's leadership. She made this demand in an article appearing in *Jenmin Jih Pao* July 13.

Regulations issued July 18 by the Chinese State Council warned that students whose thought "seriously runs against socialism face penalties ranging from corrective labor to long periods of work without pay." (Communist newspapers arriving in Hong Kong July 15–19 reported anti-government unrest at many mainland universities.)

The effects of the pressure against those who spoke against the government soon became obvious. The 2 leading non-Communist critics of the Peking régime, Timber Industry Min. Lo Lung-chi and Communications Min. Chang Po-chun, confessed July 15 to having plotted together "to attack the Communist Party and leadership." The 2 men, vice chairmen of the pro-Communist Democratic League, told the closing session of the National People's Congress that they had absorbed bourgeois ideas while studying abroad. Chang said he had sought "to replace the proletarian dictatorship and the National People's Congress with bourgeois democracy," which "would inevitably have led to a capitalist comeback" in China.

U.S. Favors Easier China Travel

The U.S. government in July 1957 announced a relaxation of the ban on visits to mainland China by American citizens. State Secy. Dulles offered July 18 to ease the State Department's ban on travel in Communist China by U.S.

newsmen. Dulles' proposal, presented to a group of U.S. news organization representatives, called for a limited number of U.S. reporters to work in China on a 6-month trial basis. Reports said that the group had rejected the plan as government intervention in news operations.

Dulles nevertheless authorized 24 news organizations Aug. 22 to send correspondents to the Chinese mainland for a 7-month trial period to report on conditions inside Communist China.

In announcing the reversal of the ban on travel to Communist China by U.S. newsmen, a State Department statement said Aug. 22 that Dulles' decision had been based on "new factors" that made it desirable that "additional information be made available to the American people respecting current conditions within China." The State Department emphasized that (a) the decision did "not change the basic policy of the [U.S.] toward communism in China"; (b) in general, travel by U.S. citizens to mainland China still was not "lawful" or "consistent with [U.S.] policy"; and (c) the U.S. "will not accord reciprocal visas to Chinese bearing passports issued by" Peking. The State Department warned that newsmen proceeding to mainland China would face "abnormal personal risks" because of the Peking government's refusal "to treat American citizens in accordance with the accepted code of civilized nations." It said, however, that the Treasury Department would be asked to issue licenses under the Trading-with-the-Enemy Act to permit the operation of the program "on an experimental basis."

Pres. David Linton of the American Society of Magazine Photographers and Robert McCandless, freedom-of-information chairman for the National Press Photographers Association, accused the State Department Aug. 25 of "drastic discrimination" for its failure to include photographers in the program.

A group of 41 young Americans toured China between August and October 1957 without U.S. government approval.

The group had left Moscow by train Aug. 14, en route to
Peking on a 3-week tour of Communist China. The 41 were
members of a 160-person U.S. delegation to the USSR's
6th World Festival of Youth & Students, held in Moscow
July 28–Aug. 11. They began the trip despite the receipt
Aug. 13 of letters from State Undersecy. Christian A. Herter
warning that a "quasi state of war" existed between the
U.S. and Communist China and that they faced passport
revocation and possible prosecution under the Trading-with-
the-Enemy Act. The State Department had charged Aug. 12
that the trip "would be subversive of [U.S.] foreign policy."

The 41 who left Moscow were part of a 50-member
group that had been invited to mainland China Aug. 7—15
of them on an all-expense basis—by the All-China Youth
Federation. In a statement issued Aug. 14, 35 of the travelers
said that they were making the trip to reaffirm "the right of
[U.S.] citizens to travel." Most of the group conceded to
U.S. correspondents in Moscow that their acceptance of the
trip had been based on its low cost and attractions as an
advanture. In an attempt to avoid U.S. penalties, the 41 received Communist Chinese visas Aug. 12–14 on documents
separate from their passports.

Reciprocity Dispute

Peking reacted with sharp criticism to Dulles' offer to
let American newsmen go to China.

In a statement published in *Jenmin Jih Pao* and broadcast by Peking radio, the Peking government Aug. 25 denounced the American plan as "completely unacceptable
to the Chinese people." The newspaper's editorial, quoted
in Hsinhua (New China) News Agency dispatches to Hong
Kong Aug. 26, charged the U.S. with "insufferable arro-
gance" in planning to "send its correspondents to China
just on the basis of its own unilateral decision," while at the
same time "refusing reciprocal visas to Chinese corre-

spondents." *Jenmin Jih Pao* accused the U.S. State Department of "placing obstacles in the way of mutual visits between the Chinese and American people" and of "trying to shift the responsibility to the Chinese government." The paper said that the State Department "wants to collect intelligence in China through its correspondents [and] carry out subversive activities." The "principle of equality and reciprocity requires that newsmen of both sides be allowed to stay in each other's country," the paper declared.

11 U.S. newsmen arrived in Hong Kong by Aug. 26 and awaited entry visas from Peking. Pressed by reporters to explain the U.S.' refusal of reciprocity and the State Department's insistence Aug. 25–26 that no Communist Chinese newsmen would be permitted to enter the U.S., Dulles said at his news conference Aug. 27 that "if any application is made" by a Chinese reporter, it would be considered "on its merits" "under the law." Dulles added: "So far as I know, we have never laid down any absolute rule that no Chinese Communist could come to this country," but there was "no application for anyone" from Communist China.

Defending the U.S.' rejection of news reciprocity with Red China, Dulles said: "We wanted to obviate any claim by the Chinese Communists that they would be entitled as a right to send a corresponding number" of newsmen to the U.S. "That we could not do under the law," which "hedges about very strictly the possibility of Communists coming to this country." "There has to be a finding made by the Attorney General to permit any Communist to come. Whether or not he could make these findings [considering current U.S.-Communist Chinese relations] I do not know," Dulles said.

Peking was adamant on the reciprocal treatment of U.S. and Chinese correspondents. At a reception given to some of the visiting American youths Sept. 6, Premier Chou En-lai said that China's "door is always open," but "it should be on an equal and mutual basis." Meeting with 10 American students Sept. 7, Chou declared that the U.S. State Department had put an end to the matter of exchanging newsmen "by refusing reciprocal rights of coverage to Chinese reporters."

The U.S. Sept. 12 rejected a formal Communist Chinese request for an agreement "to give permission to an equal and reciprocal basis for correspondents. . .to enter their respective countries for news coverage." The Chinese offer, made earlier Sept. 12 in Geneva at a meeting between Chinese Amb.-to-Poland Wang Ping-nan and U.S. Amb.-to-Czechoslovakia U. Alexis Johnson, was rejected on the ground that under U.S. law, all Chinese visa application must be considered on an individual basis. The U.S. urged that Communist China handle American newsmen's visas in the same way.

Dulles, in a letter Sept. 24 (made public Oct. 3) to J. R. Wiggins, executive editor of the *Washington Post* and *Times Herald* said that current American restrictions on travel to Communist China did not violate freedom of the press since they were applied to the general public, not just to reporters.

In the meantime, 10 of the U.S. youths who had gone to China had visited Sept. 7 with John T. Downey, 27, and Richard Fecteau, 30, U.S. civilians jailed by Communist China for allegedly dropping supplies to saboteurs in Manchuria. The students reported Sept. 8 that Fecteau, imprisoned in Peking, had admitted working for the Central Intelligence Agency when shot down on a flight from Korea to Japan in 1952. Other young Americans visited Shanghai Sept. 19 and were permitted to see 3 U.S. civilians imprisoned as spies: Hugh F. Redmond, 37, and the Rev. Joseph McCormick, 64, and the Rev. John Wagner, 50, Roman Catholic priests.

The State Department had announced Sept. 18 that it would seize the passports of all 41 students who broke U.S. passport and currency regulations to visit China. It also had said that a "final decision" had been made not to permit William Worthy, Baltimore *Afro-American* correspondent who visited China, to renew his passport.

14 of the young Americans who defied the State Department ban on travel to Communist China returned to Moscow from Peking Oct. 5 and were informed by Edward Killiam, U.S. consular official in Moscow, that their passports were valid only for return to the U.S. Shelby Tucker Jr., 22, of Pass Christian, Miss. had returned to Moscow Sept. 8 after being ordered expelled from mainland China Aug. 31 for refusing to show officials his passport. He was permitted to continue to England to resume his studies at Oxford University. Earl R. Richardson, 28, of Oakland, Calif. left China via Hong Kong Sept. 14 and relinquished his passport to U.S. officials in Honolulu Sept. 17.

TAIWAN STRAITS CRISIS OF 1958

U.S. Reaffirms Nonrecognition Policy

The Dulles-Chou duel continued through public diplomacy during the rest of 1957. In the summer of 1958, the clash of words turned into a clash of arms, and the U.S. and Communist China moved once again toward the brink of war in the Taiwan Straits.

The Sino-American ambassadorial talks in Geneva were virtually suspended in Dec. 1957, when the chief U.S. delegate, U. Alex Johnson, was transferred to Thailand as the U.S. ambassador in Bangkok. The State Department did not appoint as his successor a diplomat with ambassadorial rank, and Chinese Amb. Wang Ping-nan refused to negotiate with the first secretary who represented the U.S. The Peking government June 30, 1958 served a warning on the U.S. that it intended to break off the negotiations unless the U.S. resumed the ambassadorial talks on a level of equal diplomatic rank within 15 days.

The State Department June 30 rejected the "15-day ultimatum," denying that Washington had downgraded the ambassadorial talks by not appointing Johnson's successor. State Secy. Dulles said at a Washington news conference July 1 that the U.S. would not "pay blackmail" to secure the release of American civilians and servicemen held by Communist China, other Communist countries and left-wing insurgents in Cuba. Dulles asserted that any concession to "blackmail" would only "encourage further efforts to use Americans as hostages." Dulles told reporters that the U.S. would propose the transfer of the U.S.-Communist Chinese talks from Geneva to Warsaw after the release of 4 imprisoned Americans.

The State Department Aug. 10 made public a memo that it had sent to the U.S. embassies abroad Aug. 9. The memo reiterated the U.S. determination not to recognize the Communist Chinese government. The grounds were that "communism's rule in China is not permanent and that one day it will pass." The document added: "By withholding diplomatic recognition from...[Peking, the U.S.] seeks to hasten that passing."

The memo made clear the official U.S. opposition to the "2 Chinas" concept based on recognition of both the Communist and Nationalist (Taiwan) régimes. It said that Pres. Chiang Kai-shek's Nationalist government "would not accept any diminuation of its sovereignty over China" and that the Peking government had repeatedly rejected any solutions based on the recognition of both régimes. It asserted that continued nonrecognition would deny Communist China access to international councils, make difficult the exercise of its foreign policy and bolster those overseas Chinese and Asians who refused to accept Peking's domination.

The statement asserted, however, that nonrecognition was not an "inflexible policy which cannot be altered." It indicated that the U.S. would "readjust its present policies" if "the situation in the Far East were so to change in its basic elements as to call for a radically different evaluation of the threat Chinese Communist policies pose to [the U.S.]." But the memo made clear that a U.S. policy change was likely only if (a) Communist China renounced efforts to extend its rule through Asia, or (b) the Nationalist régime collapsed internally.

Tension Mounts Over Offshore Islands

The Peking government derided the State Department memo as "shopworn." Vowing to liberate Taiwan, Communist China built up military forces on mainland shores opposite the small islands of Quemoy and Matsu, held by Nationalist forces. Communist Chinese Foreign Min. Chen Yi was reported to have said at a diplomatic reception

Aug. 22, 1958 that "we are about to liberate" or "we have begun the liberation of Matsu and Quemoy."

Communist Chinese aircraft strafed Quemoy Aug. 24 for the first time in 1958 and continued heavy activity in the area until Aug. 26, when 2 of 48 Communist planes were shot down. The Nationalist Central News Agency said Aug. 28 that Communist marine, amphibious and torpedo-boat units had been concentrated in the mainland ports of Chusan and Santuao for a possible invasion attempt against Quemoy and Matsu islands. (The Matsu area remained inactive except for some shelling and air patrols.)

U.S. State Secy. Dulles warned Aug. 23 that any Communist Chinese attempt to seize the Nationalist-held offshore islands would constitute a "threat to the peace of the area." In a letter to Acting Chairman Thomas E. Morgan (D., Pa.) of the House Foreign Affairs Committee, Dulles conceded that the U.S. was "disturbed by the evidence of Communist Chinese buildup," which "suggests that they might be tempted to try to seize [the islands] forcibly." He reiterated that in the event of an attack on the islands, "Pres. Eisenhower will decide as to the. . .value of certain coastal positions to" Taiwan and as to whether the U.S. would aid in holding them.

The U.S. 7th Fleet was ordered Aug. 24 to take "normal precautionary defense measures" in Far Eastern waters as a result of "the increased activity" in the Taiwan Straits. An 8-vessel U.S. amphibious force carrying 1,600 Marines sailed from Singapore Aug. 26 for Okinawa and for combined maneuvers on Taiwan.

Eisenhower said at his Washington news conference Aug. 27 that the Nationalist-held offshore islands were more important to Taiwan defense than they had been 3 years previously. The President, who refused to indicate whether the U.S. would act to defend the outposts against a Communist invasion, said that "the Nationalist Chinese have now deployed about a third of their forces to. . .these islands. . ., and that makes a closer interlocking between the defense systems of the islands with Formosa than. . . before." Eisenhower said the U.S. would not "desert our responsibilities or the statements we have already made."

A radio broadcast from Peking to the Chinese Nationalist garrison on Quemoy Aug. 29 said that Communist sea, air and artillery pressure had made the island a "hopeless place" and that a Communist Chinese "landing on Quemoy is imminent." The broadcast said that the Communists were "determined to liberate Taiwan. . . as well as the offshore islands." The Quemoy garrison was served an ultimatum to "stop resistance immediately and return to the fatherland" or "be totally destroyed."

The U.S. State Department, in a statement on the Quemoy invasion threat, said Aug. 29 that the Communist broadcasts had confirmed the American view that "the offshore islands are intimately related to Taiwan." The U.S. statement warned that it would be "highly hazardous" for the Communists to assume that an attempt on their part "to change the situation by force" in the Taiwan Straits "could be a limited operation." The invasion threat and bombardment of Quemoy and its subsidiary islands were said to contradict Peking's "repeated professions of peaceful intent."

In line with this policy, moves to reinforce American forces in the Taiwan Straits area were disclosed with (a) the announcement Aug. 27 that the aircraft carrier *Essex* and 4 destroyers were being shifted to the 7th Fleet in the Taiwan Straits from the 6th Fleet in the Mediterranean; (b) the announcement Aug. 29 that the carrier *Midway* was being shifted from Hawaii to the 7th Fleet, raising the strength of the American naval force near Taiwan to 6 carriers, 2 cruisers, 36 destroyers, at least 4 submarines and more than 20 support and amphibious vessels; (c) the disclosure Aug. 30 that the U.S. Air Force in the Far East had been reinforced by a squadron of jet fighters and a number of transport planes, presumably based on Taiwan.

U.S. Army Secy. Wilbur M. Brucker and Gen. Isaac D. White, U.S. Army commander in the Pacific, conferred in Taipei Aug. 30–31 with Generalissimo Chiang Kai-shek and his chief of staff, Lt. Gen. Wang Shu-ming. Brucker said as he concluded his visit that it would "ill become the Communists to spurn the fair warnings" issued by Pres. Eisenhower (Aug. 27, for instance) against a Communist attempt to seize islands in the Taiwan Straits.

The Soviet Union voiced its support for Peking on the Taiwan Straits issue. Moscow *Pravda* said Aug. 31 that the USSR would give Communist China all "necessary moral and material aid" to overcome "aggressors" and that "American military preparations" and "aggressive intentions" were to blame for the tension in the area.

Meanwhile, Communist and Nationalist Chinese had exchanged artillery fire Aug. 29 in the Taiwan Straits; and the Tan Islands (96-acre Tatan and 40-acre Ehrtan), $2\frac{1}{2}$ miles south of Amoy port and 10 miles west of Quemoy, had been subjected to heavy Communist artillery bombardment. Tungting, a 40-acre island 17 miles south of Quemoy, became the next principal target for bombardment Aug. 31. It was disclosed Aug. 31 that the Communists had established a group of MIG-17 jet fighter planes on a new airstrip at Shati, 9 minutes' flying time from the Pescadores' Penghu Island.

The Nationalists reported that their batteries on Quemoy had shelled a concentration of Communist gunboats and motorized junks near Amoy Sept. 1, sinking 3 gunboats and 8 junks. A clash between the light naval forces of the rival Chinese developed Sept. 2 when Communist torpedo boats raided Liaolo Bay off Quemoy to turn back 2 landing-craft supply boats bound from Taiwan to Quemoy. 4 Nationalist corvettes were said to have intercepted the raid, sunk 5 Communist torpedo boats and set 6 others afire. 9 of about 30 newsmen in the Quemoy-bound convoy got ashore aboard harbor craft.

Dulles Implies Threat of Attack on Mainland

Amid speculation over what action the U.S. would take if Communist China invaded Quemoy, Pres. Eisenhower Sept. 2, 1958 called State Secy. Dulles to his vacation headquarters at Ft. Adams in Newport, R.I. Dulles conferred with Eisenhower Sept. 4 for 2 hours; then he issued a statement saying that the President "would not...hesitate" to order "timely and effective" military measures if he decided that a Communist Chinese attack on Quemoy and other Chinese offshore islands menaced Taiwan.

In an anonymous briefing session with reporters on the formal statement, Dulles said that the U.S. might bomb Chinese mainland concentrations of Communist forces "if Formosa was attacked or imminently threatened from those airfields." He warned that the same applied to the defense of Quemoy. Asked whether the official statement constituted a warning to the Reds not to attack Quemoy, Dulles replied: "If I were on the Communist side, I would certainly think very hard before I went ahead in the face of this statement."

Dulles made the following points in his formal statement for the record:

● Taiwan, Quemoy and Matsu "have never been under the authority of the Chinese Communists," and the Nationalists had held them since World War II.
● The U.S. had treaty obligations to help defend Taiwan, and Congress had authorized the President to insure the defense of "related positions such as Quemoy and Matsu."
● A Communist attempt to seize the islands "would be a crude violation of the principles upon which world order is based, namely, that no country should use armed force to seize new territory."
● The Communists had been bombarding Quemoy and the other offshore islands, harassing their supply lines and broadcasting threats to seize them and Taiwan.
● It was "not yet certain that their purpose is in fact to make an all-out effort to conquer" the islands, "nor that the islands could not be held" by "the courageous, and purely defensive, efforts of [Nationalist] China, with such substantial logistical support as the U.S. is providing."

● Because of this uncertainty over the Communists' real intentions and Nationalist defensive strength, "the President has not yet made any finding" under the joint Congressional resolution on Formosa's defense "that the employment of [U.S.] armed forces. . .is required or appropriate in insuring the defense of Formosa. The President would not, however, hesitate to make such a finding if he judged that the circumstances made this necessary to accomplish the purposes of the joint resolution. . . . Military dispositions have been made by the U.S. so that a Presidential determination, if made, would be followed by action both timely and effective."

● Pres. Eisenhower and Dulles "earnestly hope" that Communist China "will not again, as in the case of Korea, defy the basic principle. . .that armed force should not be used to achieve territorial ambitions." Such action against Taiwan and the offshore islands "would forecast a wide-spread use of force in the Far East which would endanger vital free-world positions and the security of the U.S. Acquiescence therein would threaten peace everywhere."

● The U.S. still advocated, as it had during the U.S.-Communist Chinese talks in Geneva from 1955 until 1958, a "mutual and reciprocal renunciation of force, except in self-defense. . .without prejudice to the pursuit of policies by peaceful means."

Dulles, speaking not for attribution (he was identified as the spokesman by ex-State Secy. Dean G. Acheson Sept. 6), then assumed the rôle of "briefing officer" and told newsmen that "we would not wait until the situation was desperate before we acted" to prevent the Communists from overrunning Nationalist forces on Quemoy and Matsu.

Acheson took issue with Dulles. In a statement issued Sept. 6, Acheson denounced the "horrendous decision" on a U.S. defense of Quemoy and Matsu. Acheson contended that the offshore islands were traditionally "controlled by the same power which controlled the adjacent [mainland] coast" and were useless except to block the mainland port of Amoy and pose an invasion menace to the mainland. "Only weakness would lead a mainland government, whatever its nature, to permit this situation to continue," he said. Acheson argued that: Congress had left it to the President to decide "the question of the common sense of war over these offshore islands"; "the principles on which world order is based. . .are not involved" in the offshore islands, which had "more effect on the security of the mainland. . .than upon that of Formosa"; the Communists would "always control the fighting" over the offshore islands, and America's involvement would fulfill both Chiang Kai-shek's goal "to embroil the U.S. with his enemies" and the Communists' desire "to drive the U.S. into conflict over an issue so unimportant as to lose us the support of all our friends"; although Congress had "been led to say" in 1953 that Taiwan's defense was vital to U.S. security, "4 times between 1948 and 1950 our highest military authorities [had] concluded that this proposition was not true."

Acheson said that by letting Chiang commit the "incredible folly" of shifting ⅓ of his forces to "untenable Quemoy," the government had been maneuvered "into a situation of which it has lost control. Either the Nationalists or the Communists, or both, can at any moment—this is one of them—precipitate us into war or back-down." The Eisenhower Administration's policy that "nothing will be done to extricate ourselves from this position during periods of quiet, and that nothing can be done about it in times of crisis...ought not to be tolerated," Acheson declared.

Peking Declares 12-Mile Limit

The Peking government Sept. 4, 1958 had issued a proclamation claiming all waters within 12 miles of its shorelines. The proclamation claimed Quemoy, Matsu and other offshore islands nearby as within its territorial seas and also applied the 12-mile limit to Taiwan, the Pescadores and other islands claimed by Communist China but separated from the mainland by the high seas. Taiwan and the Pescadores were characterized as "still occupied by the U.S. by armed force" and subject to recovery by mainland China "by all suitable means at a suitable time." All foreign military vessels and foreign aircraft were barred from entering the extended territorial sea and its air space without the Peking government's permission.

The Soviet Union voiced its support for Peking. *Izvestia*, the Soviet government's unofficial newspaper, said in an article Sept. 5 that the USSR, "in case of necessity," would "aid Red China with all possible means at its disposal, just as if its own fate were being decided." Moscow *Pravda* Sept. 5 termed the Communist claim to the Nationalist-controlled islands "lawful and just." It said that American attempts to block them by force would bring down on the U.S. "such a crushing rebuff that it will put an end to U.S. imperialist aggression in the Far East."

U.S. and British officials promptly rejected Communist China's 12-mile-limit claim and said that their governments would continue to recognize only the traditional 3-mile territorial limit. U.S. war-ships began Sept. 6 to escort Nationalist supply and ammunition convoys over the 100-mile ocean route from Taiwan to a point 3 miles off Quemoy, where Nationalist Navy escorts took over. After having denounced the American escort action on propaganda broadcasts, the Communists resumed their bombardment of Quemoy from the mainland Sept. 8–9 and sank Nationalist vessels as they approached Quemoy inside the 3-mile zone. American warships were not fired on.

Ambassadorial Talks Resumed in Warsaw

Against this background of impending clash, the U.S.-Communist Chinese ambassadorial talks were resumed, this time at Warsaw, Poland. The initiative was taken by Premier Chou En-lai in a statement Sept. 6, 1958. Chou proposed the resumption of the talks, which had been suspended since Dec. 1957, in order to seek a solution of the Taiwan problem. He defended Peking's claims that the fate of Taiwan and the offshore islands was a Chinese "internal affair." He told Communist China's 600 million people to mobilize for "struggle against war provocation by American imperialists in the Taiwan area" and promised Quemoy a respite in bombardment so that the Nationalists would have time for "reflection."

The White House responded Sept. 6 with a statement that U.S. Amb.-to-Poland Jacob D. Beam "stands ready to meet promptly" in Warsaw with Communist Chinese Amb.-to-Poland Wang Ping-nan, the Communist Chinese negotiator in the Geneva talks. (Washington had announced Aug. 3 that Beam would be the U.S. negotiator.) The statement added that the U.S. would, as in Geneva, "adhere to the negotiating position. . .that we will not. . .be a party to any arrangement which would prejudice the rights of our ally, the Republic of [Nationalist] China."

After the resumption of the ambassadorial talks had been agreed on, Soviet Premier Khrushchev sent to Pres. Eisenhower a letter declaring that "an attack on the People's Republic of China. . .is an attack on the Soviet Union." The premier's letter was made public in Moscow Sept. 8. In the letter, Khrushchev observed that the maneuvering of warships "loses today much of its sense" because "the heyday of surface navy power is over" in the age of "nuclear and rocket weapons." Khrushchev upheld Communist China's right to all Nationalist-held territory and China's seat in the UN, which, he said, remained in possession of the Nationalists only because the U.S. "still prefers to close its eyes to the real state of affairs in China."

Eisenhower defended his policy in a countrywide radio-TV address Sept. 11. He prefaced his remarks on the crisis by observing that "some misguided persons have said that Quemoy is nothing to become excited about." The President said that the Communist Chinese were using the offshore islands in the Taiwan Straits as a place for testing the free world's courage to resist aggression. The main points of his address were:

● "They [the Communist Chinese] frankly say that their present military effort [in bombarding and blockading

Quemoy and Matsu] is part of a program to conquer Formosa.... It is part of what is indeed an ambitious plan of
armed conquest" to "liquidate all of the free-world positions
in the western Pacific area and bring them under captive
governments...hostile to the U.S. and the free world.... In
this effort the Chinese Communists and the Soviet Union
appear to be working hand in hand," as evidenced by Soviet
Premier Khrushchev's letter of Sept. 8 pledging strong
Soviet support for Communist Chinese actions. If the Communist Chinese "have now decided to risk a war" over
Quemoy, "it can only be because they and their Soviet
allies have decided to find out whether threatening war is a
policy from which they can make big gains."

• A "western Pacific Munich" would "encourage the aggressors," "dismay our friends and allies there" and "make
it more likely that we would have to fight a major war" to
repel larger-scale aggression encouraged by appeasement.

• The meaning of State Secy. Dulles' Sept. 4 statement,
issued after a conference with the President, was that "there
will be no retreat in the face of armed aggression which is
part and parcel of a continuing program of using armed force
to conquer new regions." Although the use of the President's
1955 Congressional authorization (the "Formosa Resolution") to defend Quemoy and Matsu was a matter of "my
judgment according to circumstances of the time," a Communist assault on Quemoy "with which the local [Nation-
alist] defenders could not cope" would present the U.S. with
"precisely the situation that Congress visualized in 1955."
"No American boy will ever be asked by me just to fight for
Quemoy," but Americans always would "defend the principle that armed force shall not be used for aggressive
purposes."

The President, voicing hope for good results from the
forthcoming U.S.-Communist Chinese talks, said that he
doubted whether "any rulers, however aggressive,... will

flout efforts to find a peaceful and honorable solution, whether it be by direct negotiations or through the UN." "We believe that arrangements are urgently required to stop the gunfire and to pave the way to a peaceful solution." He termed the Taiwan Straits situation "serious" but not "desperate or hopeless" and asserted that "there is not going to be any war."

Ex.-Pres. Harry S. Truman gave his support to Eisenhower. Disagreeing with Dean Acheson, his former State Secretary, Truman said in a statement distributed to the press Sept. 14: "The probing tactics of the Chinese Communists over Quemoy and Matsu are part of a reckless campaign to determine whether they can get full support of the Kremlin and whether we will stand up to their use of force to take over Quemoy, Matsu and Formosa." The mission of American forces in the area was purely defensive —"to prevent any mad adventure which could set off a 3d world war"—and posed "no threat to the Chinese people or any other people." Until "there is absolute assurance that the Communists have abandoned their aim of territorial expansion, I cannot see that we have any other choice but to meet them and thwart them at every point where it is necessary. It would be folly and dangerous for us to abandon Formosa to the Communists as long as they are aggression-minded. . . . Formosa could be the launching point for Communist assaults on the Philippines, Korea and Japan. . . ."

The British Foreign Office Sept. 12 had issued a statement supporting Eisenhower's call for a negotiated settlement. Speaking at the Conservative Party meeting in Bromley Sept. 12, British Prime Min. Harold Macmillan said that the U.S. had "neither sought nor received promises of military support from us in the Formosa area." This fact, he said, obligated Britain "to help in any way we can, by private consultation and public action, to secure a peaceful solution" to the Taiwan Straits problem. A British Foreign

Office spokesman had said earlier Sept. 12 that the British government "strongly approved" Eisenhower's call for a negotiated settlement.

Macmillan Sept. 15 rejected a plea by Labor Party leader Hugh Gaitskell that the British government inform the U.S. that Britain would not fight in a war that started over Quemoy. "We would be playing into the hands of the Communists if we allowed ourselves to take public attitudes on difficulties which we hope jointly to overcome," Macmillan replied. Gaitskell, addressing the (British) Foreign Press Association in London Sept. 16, reiterated his demand for British neutrality. He said that the Chinese Communists, although claiming the offshore islands, had "for 3 years . . . refrained from using force in the hope that Chiang would withdraw."

Eisenhower replied Sept. 13 to Khrushchev's letter of Sept. 8. In his reply, Eisenhower denied that the U.S. or Nationalist China were to blame for the renewal of tension in the Taiwan area or that the U.S. forces there were aggressive. The President said that the Communist Chinese had broken "a long period of relative calm" by launching "without provocation" their bombardment of Quemoy and advertising their intention to take Quemoy and Matsu as stepping stones to Formosa.

Eisenhower told Khrushchev that American forces were fulfilling treaty obligations to Nationalist China "to assist it in the defense of" Taiwan and the Pescadores and that "no upside-down presentation such as contained in your letter can change this fact." He challenged Khrushchev to "urge these [Communist Chinese] leaders to discontinue their military operations and turn to a policy of peaceful settlement of the Taiwan dispute."

While preparing for ambassadorial talks, the U.S. sought to improve its bargaining position by bringing relief to the Chinese Nationalist forces on the offshore islands.

Thus, after a week of isolation due to storms and Communist bombardment that kept convoys away, Quemoy received a shipment of food and ammunition Sept. 14 when an LST ran through artillery fire from mainland batteries. The shipment was augmented by an air-drop of supplies by 4 Nationalist C-46 planes later Sept. 14. As the air drops continued, Nationalist LST crews aided by American advisers put ashore on Quemoy the cargo of one boat Sept. 16 and 2 Sept. 17—reportedly by running the LSTs through the Red bombardment to within a mile of shore, then launching cargo-loaded amphibious tractors that reached the Quemoy beaches. The Nationalist Chinese Defense Ministry said Sept. 17 that blockade-running techniques were being developed but needed "much more improvement" before Quemoy could be assured enough volume of supplies for its garrison (100,000 men) and civilian population (50,000) to hold out.

The ambassadorial talks were resumed Sept. 15 in Warsaw. U.S. Amb.-to-Poland Beam and Communist Chinese Amb.-to-Poland Wang met for 2¾ hours in Mysliwiecki Palace, Warsaw. Although no official accounts of the discussion were given out, reports in Washington Sept. 17 said that the Communist Chinese had offered to grant Quemoy and Matsu a cease-fire if assured that the Nationalists would withdraw from the islands. Beam was said to have demanded that the Communists halt their bombardment and blockade prior to talks on a political settlement and a guarantee that the Nationalists would not strike at the mainland.

The talks continued Sept. 18 and 22. NBC-TV newscaster David Brinkley said Sept. 18 that he had information from a high Washington source that: (a) the U.S. had demanded an immediate cease-fire for Quemoy and Matsu, after which it would negotiate to have the islands neutralized through the gradual withdrawal of Nationalist troops over a period of one to 2 years; (b) Communist China held that a cease-fire did not concern the U.S. because its forces on and around the islands were not under attack, and the Communists demanded Nationalist withdrawal from Quemoy and Matsu and the withdrawal of U.S. forces from the entire Taiwan area.

Chinese Nationalists were skeptical of the Warsaw talks. In Taipei, the Nationalist spokesman Sept. 14 expressed his doubts that good results would come from the U.S.-Communist Chinese talks in Warsaw. He said that peaceful appeals to the Communists were as futile as "playing music to an ox."

Chiang Kai-shek, interviewed in Taipei Sept. 15 by N.Y. *Herald Tribune* writer Joseph Alsop, said Quemoy's garrison and population could not be sustained by convoys landing under Communist fire and that the "one real solution to the problem" was to "attack it at the source" by knocking out the Communist mainland batteries. This kind of retaliation had silenced Communist attacks in 1954, he said. He called the resumption of U.S.-Communist Chinese talks "a loss" but urged "understanding, instead of opposition or objection" toward the American desire to try to "find a peaceful settlement."

Nationalist Chinese Vice Pres.-Premier Chen Cheng told the Legislative Yuan (parliament) in Taipei Sept. 19 that the Nationalist government would "not accept any resolution reached in Warsaw that might prejudice the rights of [Nationalist] China. Nobody has the right to make us demilitarize these islands. Communist occupation of Quemoy and Matsu would pose a serious threat to the security of all the Far East area."

Fighting in Taiwan Straits

Chinese Nationalists and Communists clashed militarily in the Taiwan Straits in Sept. 1958. The Nationalist Chinese claimed the downing of at least 5 Communist MIG-17 jet planes and the sinking of at least 3 Communist torpedo boats Sept. 18 and the downing of at least 10 MIG-17s Sept. 24, all by Nationalist air force Sabrejet fighter planes operating over the Taiwan Straits between Taiwan and the mainland. The Nationalist air force was said to have avoided being drawn into combat over the mainland to deny the Communists any propaganda advantage from downing Nationalist planes there. The Nationalists conceded no plane losses of their own in the Sept. 18 and 24 dogfights. U.S. Air Force advisers on Taiwan upheld the Nationalist claims as borne out by gun camera pictures and other evidence. Continued daily landings of supplies on Quemoy from fleet-convoyed vessels and private junks were reported Sept. 18–24.

Nationalists estimated Sept. 21 that casualties (dead and injured) from the Communist bombardment of Quemoy Aug. 23-Sept. 21 totaled 3,000 civilians and 1,000 military personnel.

Adm. Harry D. Felt, U.S. Pacific commander-in-chief, said in Taipei Sept. 21 that the U.S. 7th Fleet Air Force units in the Taiwan area were "very, very strong" and "quite adequate" to deal with any drastic action that the Communists might take. Felt said Sept. 24, after a 5-hour conference with Chiang Kai-shek, that he and Chiang "have an understanding with each other" on military aspects of the Taiwan Straits situation. The admiral said that he was "not overly optimistic" about maintaining adequate supply convoys to Quemoy but that, for the present, "they are going well."

White House Rebuffs Khrushchev

Soviet Premier Nikita S. Khrushchev wrote to Pres. Eisenhower Sept. 19 his 2d letter since the offshore-islands crisis of 1958 had started. According to White House sources, the letter was "unacceptable under established international practices." The White House announced Sept. 20 that the letter was sent back unanswered. The White House statement said that the rejected communication was "replete with false accusations" and "abusive and intemperate," that it "indulges in personalities" and "contains inadmissible threats." U.S. officials indicated that the most objectionable portions of the Khrushchev letter included these remarks:

> The American naval fleets must be withdrawn from Formosa Straits and American soldiers must leave Formosa and go home.... If the U.S.... does not do this now, then no other way will be left to the people of China except the expulsion of armed forces hostile to it from its own territory, on which a *place d'armes* is being created for an attack on the Chinese People's Republic....
>
> After your [Eisenhower's] election as President..., Soviet statesmen pinned great hopes upon you.... However, the policy you are now pursuing as President has largely undermined these good feelings and to an ever greater degree strengthens our belief that the 'brink of war' policy of Mr. Dulles in fact is inseparable from your name, is associated with it.

A 2d White House statement Sept. 20 on the return of Khrushchev's letter said of the threat of Communist Chinese expulsion of U.S. forces from the Taiwan area: "It is tragic that Soviet military despotism should support the use of force to achieve expansionist ends." The statement said that "the use of such threats" would jeopardize efforts to reach a peaceful settlement through the U.S.-Communist Chinese talks in Warsaw. Khrushchev's letter was taken back to the Kremlin Sept. 21 by Richard H. Davis, U.S. chargé d'affaires in Moscow.

The USSR's official Tass news agency in Moscow said Sept. 21, in commenting on Eisenhower's rejection of Khrushchev's letter, that the U.S. would not "listen to the voice of reason" on the Taiwan dispute. The Soviet Communist Party daily *Pravda* commented that the U.S. had "lost a realistic approach to the international situation" and that Khrushchev's letter had won "ardent approval by the peace-loving forces" in the world.

UN Debates Offshore Islands Crisis

The offshore-islands problem was debated in the UN General Assembly. In his opening address to the Assembly at the beginning of its 13th annual meeting, U.S. State Secy. Dulles said Sept. 18, 1958 that the successive steps toward ending the crisis over the islands should be (1) a ceasefire, (2) the establishment of "equitable conditions which will eliminate provocations," and (3) the settlement of rival Chinese claims by peaceful means.

Soviet Forgn. Min. Andrei Gromyko then told the Assembly in his opening address Sept. 18 that tension would never be lifted in the area until American forces left and the offshore islands and Taiwan yielded to Communist China.

The U.S. forestalled in 1958 the annual move to admit Communist China to the UN through procedural maneuvers. The U.S. delegation introduced a motion that there be no discussion in the General Assembly of whether to seat Communist China. The motion was carried Sept. 19 in the Assembly's Steering Committee 12-7. The General Assembly approved the resolution by 44-28 with 9 members abstaining.

The Indian delegate, Defense Min. V. K. Krishna Menon, sought on both occassions to have the question put on the agenda for debate. He proposed also that the debate deal with whether Communists should replace Nationalists as Chinese delegates. Before acting on the U.S. resolution to postpone debate, the full Assembly voted Sept. 23 by 40-29 (12 abstentions) against the Indian proposal to put the Chinese representation issue on the agenda, and 41-29 (11 abstentions) against an Indian motion to kill the American measure for postponement.

During Assembly floor debate Sept. 22, U.S. Amb.-to-UN Henry Cabot Lodge called on the USSR to persuade Communist China to halt its "murderous" bombardment of Quemoy and Matsu. He said that the Communists "are rapidly shooting themselves—and the world—out of a chance to settle this question as it should be settled." Soviet Foreign Min. Gromyko advised the U.S. to withdraw its forces from the Taiwan Straits area and to "cease playing with fire in the Far East while it is not too late."

U.S. Suggests Compromise

In 3 statements within 6 days on the Formosa Straits situation, U.S. State Secy. Dulles in Sept. 1958 twice defended America's standing up to Communist Chinese threats of force and then suggested this way for the crisis over Quemoy to be eased with or without a formal agreement: a cease-fire should be declared, and then the U.S. would press for a reduction of Nationalist forces on the island.

In a speech at a Far East-America Council of Commerce & Industry dinner in New York Sept. 25, Dulles compared in principle the defense of Quemoy to that of West Berlin during the Soviet blockade of 1948–9. The Quemoy situation, he said, involved "not just some square miles of real estate" but rather a Chinese and Russian "Communist challenge to the basic principles of peace that armed force should not be used for aggression." He added that "our position is otherwise flexible" and that the U.S., while barring "surrender to force or the threat of force," would accept a solution that "eliminated from the situation features that could reasonably be regarded as provocative or which, to use Pres. Eisenhower's phrase, were 'a thorn on the side of peace.'"

Dulles reasserted in a speech Sept. 27 to the Atlantic Treaty Association in Boston that if the "principle of peaceful settlement is abandoned in the Far East, it is undermined everywhere." He said that the U.S. would not "become so involved in Asia that its contribution to NATO strength would be impaired" and "does not expect NATO military support in the Formosa area." "If the U.S. should give in to that arrogant demand" by Soviet Premier Khrushchev that it withdraw from Taiwan or be driven out, Dulles added, "the consequences would be felt in Western Europe."

At a press conference in Washington Sept. 30, Dulles said in response to questions that: (1) The U.S. government was "acquiescent" when Nationalist China insisted in putting

a major part of its army on Quemoy and the adjacent offshore islands; however, he thought the Nationalist action
was "rather foolish" and, should there be "a cease-fire in
the area which seemed to be reasonably dependable, I think
it would be foolish to keep these large forces on these islands."
(2) The cease-fire could be either by written or unwritten
agreement. A Communist pledge to keep it might be dependable if "circumstances could be created where. . .the
consequences of breaking this promise would be. . .undesir-
able to the Communists," such as the application of trade
sanctions against them by many nations. (3) A cease-fire
must be kept also by the Nationalists because it would be
"quite impractical [and] wrong to ask the Chinese Communists to abandon use of force if they were being attacked
by the Chinese Nationalists." (4) Questions of Nationalist
return to the mainland with Chiang Kai-shek's régime
restored there were "hypothetical." China might throw off
Communist rule through a revolt similar to the 1956 uprising
in Hungary, "primarily under local auspices and local
leadership."

Sen. Theodore F. Green (D., R.I.), chairman of the
Senate Foreign Relations Committee, questioned the Eisenhower Administration's policy in regard to the offshore-
islands defense. In a letter to the President Sept. 29, Greene
expressed his doubt "that Quemoy is vital to the defense of
either Formosa or the U.S." and his fear that "events in
the Far East may result in military involvement at the wrong
time, in the wrong place and on issues not of vital concern
to our own security, and all this without allies either in fact
or in heart," nor even with "the support of the American
people essential to successful military action."

Eisenhower replied that the U.S. would not become
"involved in military hostilities merely in defense of Quemoy
or Matsu," but, he said, it was his sole responsibility to
decide whether their defense was "required or appropriate

in assuring the defense of Formosa and the Pescadores."
He said that most friends and allies of the U.S. "would be
appalled if the U.S. were spinelessly to retreat before the
threat of Sino-Soviet armed aggression," and that to question the will of Americans to resist Communist aggression
played into the hands of Communist leaders.

Chiang Adamant on Islands

Chiang Kai-shek, at a news conference in Taipei Sept.
29, reaffirmed the Nationalists' determination to keep the
offshore islands, which, he said, had become a "shield"
against Communist aggression rather than a springboard for
invasion of the Chinese mainland. He said that the Nationalist stand on Quemoy and American protection of Taiwan
had "checkmated" Communist plans to begin a new expansionist drive to Asia by seizing the offshore islands.
He said that objections raised in the non-Communist world
against standing firm against Communist moves into the
Taiwan Straits were due to "lack of understanding of the
relation of the defense of the offshore islands to the defense
of Taiwan. . .and the security of the western Pacific as a
whole." He asserted that "talks with the Communists under
any circumstances is futile, and the Warsaw [U.S.-Com-
munist Chinese] talks are no exception."

Chiang did not agree with U.S. State Secy. Dulles on
the withdrawal of the Nationalist troops from the offshore
islands. Speaking with newsmen Oct. 1, Chiang said he was
"incredulous" at remarks attributed to Dulles Sept. 30
(that the stationing of a large Nationalist force on Quemoy
was "foolish," that the U.S. might accept an unwritten
cease-fire as grounds for reducing the Quemoy force and
that the question of Nationalist return to the mainland was
"hypothetical").

Eisenhower, at his news conference Oct. 1, said that a
Quemoy cease-fire was needed to create "an opportunity to

negotiate in good faith" and that the U.S.' basic aim was "to avoid retreat in the face of force." Dulles said Oct. 2 that he had instructed U.S. Amb.-to-Nationalist China Everett F. Drumwright to "straighten out" Nationalist "misconceptions" that the U.S. had changed its policy on Quemoy's defense.

Peking Orders Unilateral Cease-Fire

Meanwhile, U.S. Amb. Jacob Beam and Communist Chinese Amb. Wang Ping-nan met in Warsaw Sept. 24, 30 and Oct. 4—apparently without reaching any agreement. But the Peking government Oct. 6 called an unexpected 7-day Quemoy cease-fire "out of humanitarian considerations." The declaration, issued in the name of Defense Min. Peng Teh-huai, said that Nationalist supply convoys could be sent to the island unmolested. The cease-fire was offered "on condition that there be no American escort" of convoys.

In announcing the cease-fire, Peng issued a new call for direct Communist-Nationalist talks to end the 30-year "war between you and us." He contended that: neither Chinese side questioned whether Taiwan and the Pescadores, Quemoy and Matsu belonged to China; civil warfare over the offshore islands was "an internal Chinese matter" and "not a matter between China and the U.S."; the only issue between China and the U.S. is U.S. invasion and occupation of" Taiwan, the Pescadores and the Taiwan Straits, "and this should be settled through negotiations between the 2 countries, which are now being held in Warsaw"; there was "no war between [Communist] China and the U.S.," so "the question of a cease-fire does not arise" between them. As for Chinese civil strife, Peng asserted that "of all choices, peace is the best. . . . We propose that talks be held to effect a peaceful settlement." He said that Nationalist leaders "have been far too rampant" in harassing the mainland with bombings, leaflet raids and infiltration by secret agents. "Hence the firing of a few shells* just to call your [Taipei's] attention."

The Nationalist Chinese government on Taiwan, in reaction to Peng's statement, said Oct. 6 that it would observe an unofficial truce on Quemoy if the Communists ceased fire. The Nationalists, however, ruled out direct talks with the Communists because they "never will keep their word" and would make of peace talks "only another ruse to gain time." The British Foreign Office, active in diplomatic efforts to ease the Quemoy crisis, said it welcomed "any move in the direction of a relaxation of tension." Indian Defense Min. V. K. Krishna Menon, India's delegate to the UN, endorsed Peng's call for intra-Chinese peace talks.

U.S. State Secy. Dulles, returning to Washington Oct. 7 from a week's vacation, said that the Communist offer was "not easy to evaluate," but "for the moment there is a cessation of the bombing. This the U.S. has been vigorously seeking. Also, the development assures worldwide condemnation of the Chinese Communists if they again resume the fighting."

The U.S. State Department announced Oct. 8 that Communist China's "halt of attacks on the offshore islands and on resupply operations. . . suspends the military necessity" of the 7th Fleet's acting on a standing order to furnish "the escort of Chinese vessels resupplying Quemoy. . . to the extent militarily necessary." If the attacks were resumed, the State Department said, "U.S. escort activity will be resumed forthwith to the extent necessary." The department added that there had been "full consultation" between

---

*The Nationalist Chinese government had estimated Oct. 4 that Communist forces had fired 420,000 shells of artillery ammunition during the 42-day bombardment until then of Quemoy and Matsu islands.

the U.S. and Nationalist Chinese governments on the U.S.' response to the Communist offer.

Nationalist armed forces took advantage of the first 7-day truce to reinforce Quemoy defenses and stockpile food, munitions and equipment on the islands. Nationalist ships and aircraft traveled unescorted and were not molested by Communist shore batteries. Vessels returning to Taiwan took with them 6,000 of Quemoy's 47,000 civilians, mostly aged persons and children.

5 MIGs and one Nationalist F-86 Sabrejet were shot down when Nationalist and Communist fighter patrols clashed over Matsu Island Oct. 10, according to accounts from Taiwan. (The Communists claimed to have downed 3 Sabrejets.) The battle had no effect on the Quemoy-area truce.

The U.S. State Department announced Oct. 9 that Amb. Jacob Beam had been instructed to press for a continuation of the Quemoy cease-fire. He was to do so at his Warsaw meetings with Communist Chinese Amb. Wang Ping-nan. State Department press officer Lincoln White told newsmen that "our whole purpose" in continuing the Warsaw talks was to broaden the truce.

White charged Oct. 10 that Communist China had leaked distorted accounts of the secret Warsaw talks in an effort to escape blame for the Quemoy crisis. He denied reports appearing in the *N.Y. Times* Oct. 10 that the 7-day Quemoy truce had been preceded by a Communist Chinese offer, transmitted through the Norwegian delegation to the UN, "to negotiate an interim settlement of hostilities that would be confined to the offshore islands." The *Times* accounts said that the U.S.' response had been contained in State Secy. Dulles' Sept. 30 news conference statement that the U.S. would favor a cut in Nationalist garrisons on Quemoy and Matsu if the Communist bombardment was halted.

Peking Extends Quemoy Truce

The halt in the Communist Chinese artillery bombardment of Nationalist-held Quemoy Island was extended Oct. 12–13 for an additional 2 weeks. A Peking radio broadcast said that Defense Min. Peng Teh-huai had delayed the resumption of shelling "to see what the opposite side is going to do and enable our compatriots on Quemoy, both military and civilian, to get sufficient supplies, including food and military equipment."

Informed of the extension of the cease-fire, while he was visiting New York Oct. 12, Pres. Eisenhower called it "good news" and said in a White House statement later that day that it would afford the U.S. "a further opportunity to work out through negotiation a settlement of the problem in that area." Questioned by newsmen, Presidential Press Secy. James C. Hagerty said that the U.S. would undertake "negotiations with all sides" in an effort to end the Quemoy crisis.

The Communist order of Oct. 12-13 made clear that the truce extension was "directed against the Americans" in an effort to draw "a clear-cut line between the Chinese and the Americans." The Communist Chinese asserted that the U.S. was maintaining forces in the Taiwan area in an effort to "take a hand in our civil war." It warned that the Quemoy bombardment would "start at once" if the U.S. resumed "escort operations in the Quemoy water area." The statement conceded that Communist China had planned "off and on" fighting in the Quemoy area in an attempt to force the Nationalist government "into peaceful negotiations with us." It warned that "fighting is unavoidable" as long as the Nationalists refused to negotiate. It asserted that "the majority" of Chinese on Taiwan and the offshore islands were "patriots" who would "wake up gradually" and "isolate the handful of traitors."

Peking Resumes Shelling

U.S. State Secy. Dulles was ordered by Pres. Eisenhower
to go to Taiwan to confer with Generalissimo Chiang Kai-
shek on the defense of the offshore islands. While Dulles
was en route to Taiwan, Communist China Oct. 20 resumed
its bombardment of Nationalist-held Quemoy, Tatan, Erhtan
and Hutzu islands off the Fukien Province coast of the
Chinese mainland.

A Peking radio broadcast, monitored shortly before the
shelling was resumed, asserted that the self-imposed Communist cease-fire had been broken because of a U.S. naval
escort of a Nationalist convoy in Quemoy waters Oct. 19.
Peking termed the renewed shelling "a measure of punishment" for the alleged U.S. naval action. It renewed warnings
that Communist China considered it "absolutely imper-
missible for the Americans to meddle in internal Chinese
affairs."

The U.S.' Taiwan Defense Command denied Oct. 21
that any American vessels had entered Quemoy waters or
had acted as escort for Nationalist supply ships. American
and Nationalist authorities conceded later that a U.S. LSD
had sheltered 3 small Nationalist supply ships and that an
American destroyer had been near Quemoy Oct. 19. They
denied that either vessel had approached the 12-mile territorial limit claimed by Communist China (and not recognized by the U.S.).

Communist shore batteries hurled 11,520 shells at the
offshore islands in the first 2½ hours of renewed shelling
Oct. 20. They continued firing thereafter.

Dulles & Chiang Bar Mainland Invasion

U.S. State Secy. Dulles arrived in Taipei Oct. 20. He
authorized Oct. 22 a statement by U.S. Amb. Everett F.
Drumwright warning Communist China that the U.S. would

resume its naval escort of Nationalist vessels to the Quemoy area if such a move became militarily necessary. A naval spokesman, however, confirmed an Oct. 21 State Department announcement that such a naval escort would not be necessary because of the Nationalists' success.

Dulles and Nationalist Pres. Chiang Kai-shek Oct. 23 announced an agreement on a Nationalist pledge not to use military force to return to the Chinese mainland. A joint statement issued by Chiang and Dulles after 3 days of talks declared that the Nationalist government "considers that the restoration of freedom to its people on the mainland is its sacred mission. . . . and that the principal means of successfully achieving its mission is the implementation of Dr. Sun Yat-sen's 3 People's Principles [nationalism, democracy and social well-being] and not the use of force."

The communiqué made clear that the U.S. would continue to recognize the Nationalist government as "the authentic spokesman for Free China." It asserted that the Quemoy bombardment had served only to draw the U.S. and Nationalist government "closer together." It renewed the American agreement to consider "the defense of the Quemoys, together with the Matsus," as "closely related to the defense of Taiwan and Penghu [in the Pescadores]."

Newsmen and observers in Taipei reported that Dulles had made clear to Chiang that the U.S. would not lend military or logistic support to any Nationalist invasion of the Chinese mainland but would continue its support of existing Nationalist positions on Taiwan and the offshore islands. He was said to have persuaded Chiang to make a public renunciation of force to facilitate a renewal of the unofficial Nationalist-Communist truce in the Taiwan Straits. Dulles also was said to have won Chiang's agreement to a gradual reduction of offshore garrisons after the cessation of the current Communist bombardment.

Dulles, in a statement issued Oct. 24 after he had returned

to Washington and reported to Pres. Eisenhower, said that he at last was "confident that the Chinese Communists will not gain their ends either through their military efforts or their propaganda guile." He asserted that free Asian nations had been "heartened" by the U.S.' refusal to "retreat in the face of armed aggression."

Peking Orders Partial Cease-Fire

Marshal Peng Teh-huai, the Communist Chinese defense minister, announced in a broadcast Oct. 25 that he had ordered a new partial cease-fire "so that our compatriots, both military and civilian, on the...islands of Greater Quemoy, Tatan, Erhtan and the others may all get sufficient supplies...to facilitate your entrenchment for a long time to come." The mainland batteries were ordered to halt their bombardment of Quemoy and nearby Nationalist-held islands on even-numbered days of the month.

Peng, who addressed his message to "compatriots in Taiwan," said that Communist guns would "not necessarily conduct shelling on odd dates," but he urged Nationalists to confine their supply operations to even days "to avoid possible losses." He warned that the truce would be suspended if U.S. naval vessels resumed escort duties in Quemoy waters.

Following Peng's announcement, mainland artillery continued sporadic bombardment of the Quemoy area, but the shelling was directed away from harbor and supply areas and was reported to be light.

In its 39th and 40th "warnings" of U.S. aggression against the mainland, Communist China charged Oct. 22 that American aircraft and ships had entered Chinese air space and waters off Fukien and Kwantung Provinces.

The Communist declaration of a partial truce in the Quemoy area was denounced by U.S. State Secy. Dulles Oct. 28 as "outlandish" and "uncivilized" and a stratagem concocted "to save face" after it became clear that "the islands could not be cut off and made to wither on the vine." Dulles said that the Communists' declared willingness to shell the islands on alternate days showed that "the killing is done for political reasons and promiscuously."

Stalemate Continues Past Crisis

Communist artillery on the Chinese mainland continued the alternate-day bombardment of Quemoy and the offshore islands through the balance of 1958, firing a post-truce high of 4,057 shells Dec. 23. Nationalist army reports Nov. 23 listed a total of 576,636 Communist shells hurled at the islands in the first 3 months of the renewed bombardment. They claimed that Nationalist counter-fire had destroyed 213 Communist guns during the same period.

With the unilateral declaration by Communist China of its alternate-day cease-fire, the Taiwan Straits crisis had subsided. But the developments had done nothing to resolve the issues that had brought the U.S. and Communist China to the brink of war. Pres. Eisenhower, speaking at his Nov. 5, 1958 press conference, made clear that the U.S. would not recognize Communist China while it "continues to do . . . things which we cannot possibly stomach." Conceding that factors responsible for non-recognition of Communist China might "gradually change," the President cited Peking's continued refusal to honor an agreement to return U.S. citizens "illegally held" in Chinese prisons.

Eisenhower reassured the Chinese Nationalists Nov. 9 that the U.S. never would "retreat in the face of armed aggression" by Communist China. His assurance was given in a letter to the Taiwan Chapter of the Asian Peoples' Anti-Communist League. (The letter was written by Acting Assistant State Secy. J. Graham Parsons at the President's direction.) The message emphasized Eisenhower's previous statements that the U.S. would "not be a party to any arrangement which would prejudice the rights of our ally, the Republic of China."

State Secy. Dulles asserted Nov. 13 that Communist China was courting disaster by its efforts to create "a vast slave state to enhance the power of the international Communist movement." Dulles said that Communist attempts to make a "great leap forward" industrially had "obliterated" the individual Chinese under a "backward system of mass slavery."

In Taipei, Nationalist Premier Chen Cheng predicted Nov. 12 that the Chinese people eventually would be liberated from Communist rule by a Nationalist "counterattack" against the mainland. Speaking at a Taipei meeting attended by Pres. Chiang, Chen said: "As long as our compatriots on the mainland suffer under the [Communist] yoke . . . , we can never relax our efforts to deliver them. We are determined to . . . sacrifice our lives if need be to counterattack the mainland." Chen's pledge apparently was regarded as within the scope of the Nationalist renunciation of the use of force to regain the Chinese mainland.

Meanwhile, the Peking government hardened its attitude toward the U.S. *Jenmin Jih Pao* Oct. 27 published a collection of articles and speeches in which Chinese Communist Party Chairman Mao Tse-tung proclaimed that the forces of revolution had outstripped the forces of imperialism and reactionaries. It popularized the slogan: "All imperialists and reactionaries are paper tigers."

Communist Chinese Foreign Min. Chen Yi, in an interview with a correspondent of the *Montreal Star* Nov. 1, declared that his government was determined to liberate Taiwan and the offshore islands by one means or another. Chen said: "Quemoy, Matsu, Formosa, and the Pescadores must be liberated as a whole. We will not allow the handing over of Quemoy in exchange for placing Formosa under [UN] trusteeship," which "would be demilitarization or referring the matter to the [UN] or the International Court of Justice."

Later that month, according to reports from Taiwan Nov. 22, Nationalist leaders received Communist peace offers written by Chang Hsih-chao, a former member of the Nationalists' National Political Council currently living in Hong Kong. Chang, reportedly acting as an agent of Mao Tse-tung, was said to have urged Nationalist leaders to accept a negotiated Taiwan settlement in exchange for a promise of "fair treatment" and high positions in the Communist régime. He warned that the Nationalists eventually would face a withdrawal of U.S. forces from the Taiwan area and the annexation of Taiwan by the Peking government.

Nationalist Premier Chen Cheng confirmed Nov. 17 that Nationalist leaders had received Communist peace offers through letters and radio but had rejected them. He dismissed the peace feelers as a "Communist trick."

The U.S. government was seeking through negotiations in Warsaw a cease-fire agreement similar to the one that had ended the fighting in Korea and Indochina. U.S. State Secy. Dulles said Nov. 18: "We are now negotiating to end the hostilities in the Formosa area.... We seek reciprocal renunciation of dependence upon force to achieve political objectives."

By then an impasse had developed in the Warsaw ambassadorial talks. Communist Chinese Amb. Wang Ping-nan consistently rejected the U.S. proposal for a cease-fire as a precondition for negotiations on the status of the offshore islands. He pointed out repeatedly that Communist China was not at war with the U.S. and that, hence, there was no need for a cease-fire agreement. The U.S. must withdraw from Taiwan, a territory of China, and leave the Chinese to solve their internal problems themselves, Wang held.

Dulles made his last public statement on Communist China (before his death in the spring of 1959) in a speech delivered at San Francisco Dec. 4. He declared that the Communist shelling of Nationalist offshore islands had made it "ever more clear" that any U.S. recognition of the Communist Chinese government would deal "a well-nigh mortal blow to the survival of the non-Communist governments of the Far East." Dulles rebutted proposals that the U.S. seek to open trade relations with Communist China. He warned that for "a few millions of dollars of unreliable [mainland Chinese] trade" the U.S. would "jeopardize exports of $2½ billion" to other Far Eastern countries. Dulles conceded, however, that the U.S. would deal with mainland China whenever such action was expedient. The U.S. did not recognize Communist China, but "we do not pretend that it does not exist," he said. He warned that Communist China was "feverishly imposing a communization program designed quickly to transform the Chinese nation into a great industrial power. The program is one of slave labor," but "it is producing material results."

Communist China's refusal to discuss a settlement of the Quemoy-Matsu offshore islands dispute was disclosed to the U.S. Senate Disarmament Subcommittee Feb. 23 by Water S. Robertson, Assistant State Secretary for Far Eastern affairs. In testifying on the need for the inclusion of mainland China in any "sound and workable" disarmament pact or nuclear test ban, Robertson said that Communist China, in Warsaw negotiations with U.S. Amb.-to-Poland Jacob Beam, had refused to "negotiate on the offshore islands because to them the offshore islands are peanuts." "What they want," he warned, "is to get rid of a rival Chinese government on Taiwan. Their *sine qua non* is that we get out of the Taiwan Straits and . . . out of the Western Pacific."

BORDER PROBLEMS & SINO-SOVIET RIFT (1959-60)

Detente Efforts & New Far East Crisis

U.S. State Secy. John Foster Dulles retired Apr. 15, 1959, because of a fatal illness, as events in Tibet and Laos caused new tensions between the U.S. and Communist China.

Under Dulles' successor, Christian A. Herter, the State Department resumed the effort to negotiate the exchange of newspaper correspondents. The department announced Apr. 23 that the passports to China that had been issued to 33 U.S. journalists would be extended for another year. The announcement also stated that *bona fide* newspaper correspondents from Communist China would be eligible for a visa through a special waiver under law—on an individually selected basis.

U.S. Amb.-to-Poland Jacob D. Beam May 19, at the Warsaw ambassadorial talks with Communist Chinese Amb. Wang Ping-nan, brought up the subject of exchanging correspondents. Wang repeated Peking's previously announced requirement: the exchange of correspondents in equal numbers without conditions. He took exception to the U.S. proposal to admit Communist Chinese correspondents through special waivers. The question remained on the agenda of talks for several months with no apparent progress toward a meeting of minds.

Meanwhile, U.S. relations with Communist China took a turn for the worse with Communist China's suppression of a Tibetan rebellion and the resumption of civil war in Laos.

Tibetan Rebellion & Its Aftermath

The revolt in Tibet took place in Mar. 1959.

A country of plateau and rugged mountains, Tibet lies at the crossroads of trade and culture between China and

115

the Indian subcontinent. Historically, it had been a dependency of China; its government had enjoyed a large measure of autonomy while acknowledging the suzerainty of the Chinese government. In an apparent effort to reaffirm this historic relationship, Communist Chinese forces invaded Tibet in 1950, and a Sino-Tibetan treaty was concluded in 1951.

Subsequently, extensive reforms were introduced under the aegis of the Communist Chinese army stationed in Lhasa, the capital of Tibet. These reforms, the avowed purpose of which was to transform Tibet into a Socialist society, produced widespread resentment and were met frequently with armed resistance on the part of Tibetan tribes.

An armed clash erupted in Lhasa between Communist Chinese troops and Tibetans in Mar. 1959. The Dalai Lama, the temporal and spiritual ruler of Tibet, fled to India with an entourage consisting of his family and followers.

In India June 21, the Dalai Lama issued a statement charging Communist China with crimes of genocide against the Tibetans. He announced in August that he would take the case to the UN in order to get "civilized countries" to aid "our cause."

The Dalai Lama formally appealed to UN Secy. Gen. Dag Hammarskjöld Sept. 9 for "immediate intervention" by the UN to save Tibet from destruction by mainland China. His message urged the UN General Assembly to resume its consideration of the Tibetan issue begun when the Chinese Communists invaded Tibet in 1950. It charged Communist China with the following "offenses against the universal laws of international conduct": (1) the seizure of Tibetans' property; (2) the forcing of men, women and children into "labor gangs"; (3) "cruel and inhuman measures for. . .sterilizing Tibetan men and women with the view to the total extermination of the Tibetan race"; (4) the massacre of "thousands of innocent people"; (5) the "murder of leading citizens of Tibet"; (6) efforts to "destroy our religion and culture."

The Tibetan rebellion had elicited public interest and sympathy in the U.S. The State Department responded to the Dalai Lama's plea with a public statement, issued Sept. 10, that the U.S. government supported "the initiative of the Dalai Lama in bringing the plight of the Tibetan people directly to the attention of the United Nations." The U.S. statement urged a UN hearing for the Dalai Lama but did not indicate a renunciation of the U.S.' traditional view that Tibet was an autonomous area under Chinese suzerainty.

The Indian government of Prime Min. Jawaharlal Nehru regarded the Tibetan rebellion as an internal matter of China and therefore beyond the pale of international concern. Nehru sought to discourage the Dalai Lama's appeal to the UN. Nehru's countrymen, however, overtly sympathized with the Tibetan cause and criticized the Chinese activities in Tibet. The Chinese Communists retorted with a violent press campaign against the Indian "expansionists," who were accused by the Communist Chinese press of acting as heirs to British imperialists.

Thus, in the aftermath of the Tibetan rebellion, Sino-Indian relations became strained. Armed incidents took place along the 2,000 miles of frontiers that China shared with India along the Himalayas. In the northwest, the Communist Chinese army occupied Ladakh, a part of the disputed Kashmir state. In the northeast section, the Peking government claimed some 32,000 square miles of territory south of the McMahon Line, which had been established under the Simla agreement of 1914, signed by China, India and Tibet but not ratified by China.

An Indian government White Paper issued Sept. 7 disclosed that a Communist Chinese note had repudiated the McMahon Line Jan. 23 as a "product of British policy of aggression against the Tibet region of China." The Chinese note, signed by Premier Chou En-lai, had asserted that the "Sino-Indian boundary had never been formally delimitated" or agreed to by the Chinese and Indian governments.

Nehru told the Indian parliament Sept. 10 that Chinese claims against India had grown "gradually more rigid" during the past weeks. Nehru disclosed that 4 Chinese notes delivered Sept. 2 and 7 had accused India of "aggression" for stationing patrols at points in the North East Frontier Agency and the Bara Hoti area of Uttar Pradesh.

The Soviet government had called on China and India Sept. 9 to settle their "frontier incident" in "the spirit of friendship." A statement issued by Tass in the name of "leading Soviet quarters" appealed to Chinese and Indian leaders to thwart efforts to divide the Asian states and intensify the cold war "just before the [planned] exchange of visits between Soviet Premier Khrushchev and Pres. Eisenhower." It charged that "certain political circles and the press in the West. . ., especially in the United States," were trying to use the Chinese-Indian dispute to "create obstacles" to reducing world tension.

Resumption of Civil Strife in Laos

Laos, the smallest of the 3 countries in the territory that until Aug. 1954 was called French Indochina, had been a theater of civil war during the "first Indochinese war" (1946–54). The civil strife had been brought to an end through the establishment of a coalition régime under the Geneva Agreement of 1954.

The coalition government was short-lived. In July 1958, Premier Prince Souvana Phouma resigned because of difficulties he had had with the Communist-dominated Pathet Laos. A drift toward the right occurred under his successor, Premier Phoui Sananikone, who formed his cabinet without the participation of Pathet Laos representatives.

Fighting resumed in Laos' northeastern provinces in the summer of 1959. The Laotian government charged July 30 that an invasion by guerrilla forces from North Vietnam had occurred. The UN Scurity Council agreed Sept. 8 to look into the Laotian charges.

Hanoi radio Aug. 16 broadcast the rebel claims that the guerrillas had "liberated" "vast areas" of 4 Laotian provinces. The Hanoi reports, based on the Aug. 11 issue of *Lao Hakhat*, publication of the Laotian Neo Haksat party, the new political arm of the Pathet Laos, said that rebels controlled Muong Song and 4 other districts of Samneua Province, the Muong Nga district of Phongsaly Province and parts of Luang Prabang and Thakhek Provinces.

The U.S. State Department charged Aug. 11 that the renewed fighting in Laos had been fomented by Communist nations and might be part of a new Communist effort to keep "tensions alive in Southeast Asia." The State Department statement accused North Vietnam of directly aiding the guerrillas and hinted that the entire Laotian campaign had been with Soviet complicity. It noted that 2 members of the North Vietnam Communist Party Central Committee had conferred not long before then with Soviet First Deputy Premier Anastas I. Mikoyan in Moscow. It said that although "there seems to have been a lull in the fighting" and Laotian troops apparently had recaptured many posts initially lost to guerrillas, rebel forces included "a number of company-sized groups located in areas where their supply can come only from [the] Communists in North Vietnam."

Laotian Defense Secy. Phoumi Nosavan reported Aug. 13 that the main body of regular rebel troops had withdrawn into North Vietnamese territory, leaving 1,200 guerrillas behind. 800 of them were said to be located in Samneua Province, south of the Dienbienphu military region of North Vietnam. Laotian troops were said to be hunting 250 more guerrillas in Sanvannakhet Province and 106 escaped Pathet Lao prisoners near Muong Neu.

Laotian Premier Phoui Sananikone warned the Chinese Communists Aug. 14 that "they were wrong if they think Laos can be intimidated" and drawn into the Communist bloc. Speaking at a rally in Vientiane, Phoui charged that the Communist countries bordering on Laos had launched the attack in order to "make us one of them."

Peking blamed the U.S. for the resumption of fighting in Laos. A Communist Chinese Foreign Ministry statement broadcast Aug. 12 by Peking radio charged that the strife in Laos was "engineered from first to last by the United States." It said that the U.S. had "incited" the Laotian government to join in a Franco-U.S. agreement for the entry of a "large number of American military personnel" into Laos to "control the Laotian army" and draw Laos into "the aggressive SEATO bloc." It demanded the withdrawal of all U.S. military personnel and the abolition of "all United States military bases" in Laos.

The Soviet government charged Aug. 17 that, by permitting the entry of U.S. military personnel, Laos had violated the 1954 Geneva armistice accords establishing Laos as an independent and neutral state. The Soviet Foreign Ministry statement, issued via the Tass news agency, warned that the current Laotian strife threatened to result in full-scale civil war and become a menace to "peace in Southeast Asia." The statement demanded the reactivation of the International Control Commission for Laos, set up by the 1954 Indochinese armistice agreements but expelled by Laos in 1958 as pro-Communist. It rejected, as a "clumsy attempt to shift the blame," Laotian charges that the current guerrilla fighting had been caused by Communist China and North Vietnam.

The USSR charged that Laos, "despite its [neutrality] obligation under the Geneva agreement, has concluded a treaty legalizing the presence of United States military personnel in Laos and handing over control of the Laotian army to [them]." It said that Laos further had violated its neutrality by maintaining liaison with the "aggressive

[SEATO] bloc" and by permitting "military preparations," including the construction of U.S. air bases, for aggression against Communist China and North Vietnam. The Soviet Union proposed the reconvening of the Geneva conference to deal with the Laotian situation.

The U.S. opposed the Soviet proposal. The Laotian charges of invasion by North Vietnam were taken before the UN Security Council instead.

U.S. State Secy. Christian A. Herter Sept. 17, 1959 made clear the U.S.' determination to aid Laos against attacks by Communist rebels supported by North Vietnam. Addressing the UN General Assembly, Herter said: The U.S. "is pledged under the [UN] Charter to resist aggression. It will fulfill this pledge without equivocation. We will support the royal Laotian government in its own efforts to preserve independence."

Herter rejected Soviet calls for a new Geneva conference to deal with Laos as a "disruptive" attempt to "ignore the authority of the United Nations" and the Security Council Subcommittee on Laos. Opposing the admission of Communist China to the UN, Herter charged that the Peking régime was "supporting efforts to subvert the will of the free people of Laos." (Herter also said that the UN should "speak out in clear terms" on the "brutal Chinese Communist repression of the fundamental human rights of the Tibetans.")

The UN Security Council Subcommittee on Laos Oct. 12 ended a month-long study of the Laotian rebellion and returned to New York to prepare a report on charges that North Vietnam had armed and led the Communist rebellion in Laos. Japanese informants reported Oct. 14 that Shinichi Shibusawa, subcommittee chairman, had uncovered proof that the Laotian rebels were under the direct supervision of Marshal Peng Teh-huai, former Communist Chinese defense minister and commander of Chinese troops during the Korean war. UN sources said Oct. 20 that the subcommittee had found that North Vietnam had supplied rebels with arms and uniforms but had not found evidence that North Vietnamese troops were fighting in Laos.

Khrushchev Tries Personal Diplomacy

The Indian-Chinese border dispute and the Laotian situation, added to the unresolved Taiwan Straits crisis, aggravated U.S. relations with Communist China. The Peking government was uncompromising in its refusal to negotiate with the U.S. on any pending issues except on its own terms. In the fall of 1959, Soviet Premier Nikita S. Khrushchev apparently sought to ease the tension through personal diplomacy on the highest ("summit") level of government in Washington and Peking.

Khrushchev visited the U.S. on his own initiative Sept. 15-29. Before meeting with Pres. Dwight Eisenhower at the President's weekend resort, Camp David, Khrushchev toured the U.S., coast to coast. The Soviet premier returned to Washington Sept. 24, attended a Soviet embassy diplomatic reception and then met with a small group of business leaders at a dinner given by Eric Ridder, publisher of the *Journal of Commerce*. He told Vice Pres. Richard Nixon at the Soviet embassy that U.S. policies were "like an iceberg." He reportedly told the businessmen that he was convinced the American people wanted peace but that the U.S. government had to prove its good intentions by trade and disarmament accords with the USSR.

Khrushchev toured government facilities in the Washington area and lunched with State Secy. Christian Herter Sept. 25 before flying by helicopter to Camp David with Eisenhower. Khrushchev told Herter that "we in our country have differences, as you do, but you dramatize yours more than we do." He admitted, however, that "there have been cases where [Soviet] differences assumed dramatic form.... All here realize what I mean."

At Camp David, Khrushchev and Eisenhower conferred privately through interpreters. A joint communiqué issued Sept. 27 stated that the 2 leaders agreed on the proposition that "all outstanding international questions should be settled not by application of force but by peaceful means through negotiations."

Khrushchev returned to Moscow and then flew to Peking to attend celebrations of Communist China's 10th anniversary. His departure for China came less than 31 hours after he returned to Moscow from his U.S. visit and talks with Eisenhower. Arriving in Peking Sept. 30 aboard his TU-114 turboprop airliner, Khrushchev told welcoming Communist Chinese leaders, including Pres. Liu Shao-chi, Premier Chou En-lai and Communist Party Chairman Mao Tse-tung, that "we must make all efforts to create conditions for the establishment of world peace." Khrushchev termed his visit to the U.S. and talks with Eisenhower "valuable." He told the Chinese that he and the President had "frankly discussed big problems which we must solve and [had] tried to create an atmosphere for cooperation and peaceful co-existence, thereby contributing to . . . peace."

Speaking at a Peking banquet in his honor, Khrushchev, in a presumed warning to Chinese leaders, said Sept. 30: "We [Soviet-bloc nations] . . . must do everything possible to preclude war as a means for settling outstanding questions"; although the Communist nations had "created a mighty potential," "this certainly does not mean that . . . we should test the stability of the capitalist system by force"; "even such a noble and progressive system as socialism cannot be imposed by force of arms against the will of the people"; "this would be wrong," and "the peoples would never understand and would never support [it]."

Premier Chou said at the banquet that the Soviet leader had succeeded in his mission as "an envoy of peace." He declared that Chinese leaders "welcome[d] the communiqué" with which Khrushchev and Eisenhower had ended their Camp David talks.

Communist China marked its 10th anniversary Oct. 1 with a parade of hundreds of thousands of troops and civilians through Peking's Square of Heavenly Peace. The parade was reviewed by Khrushchev, Mao and other Chinese and Soviet-bloc leaders. The parade included a fly-by of 45 jet bombers and 100 jet fighters, all described as Chinese-built.

Speaking at a Peking rally Sept. 28, Pres. Liu had complained that the U.S. "still occupies our territory, Taiwan," and warned that Communist China "absolutely could not tolerate" this situation. "We Chinese people," he declared, "are determined to liberate our territory of Taiwan, Penghu [in the Pescadores], Quemoy and Matsu." He lauded the Communist commitment to coexistence of states with differing social systems, but he asserted that, "on the other hand, to safeguard peace we must curb aggression."

The threat to use force to end the Nationalist rule of Taiwan was repeated Oct. 1 by Marshal Lin Piao, Communist Chinese defense minister, in an address at the Peking military parade. Lin pledged that China would "never invade anyone nor. . .allow anyone to invade us," but he asserted that China would "liberate" Taiwan "in one way or another" and that no foreign power could prevent it.

Foreign Min. Chen Yi, in an article written for Moscow's *Izvestia* and reprinted Oct. 4 by *Jenmin Jih Pao*, said that in the 10 years since Communist China's birth, U.S. "imperialists have carried out a series of aggressive acts and war threats against new China, fully revealing that they are the enemy of the Chinese people." He charged that despite a lessening of East-West tension, "up to the present the United States has not renounced its policy of aggression and war." Chen denounced the U.S.' rôle in Korea and Taiwan and the "scheme of creating 2 Chinas." "We firmly demand that American troops pull out of the Taiwan area," he said.

"Taiwan is Chinese territory, and the Chinese people are determined to liberate it."

During his 4-day stay in Peking, Khrushchev, accompanied by Soviet Foreign Min. Andrei Gromyko, held a series of secret talks with Mao Tse-tung, Liu Shao-chi and Chou En-lai. No joint communiqué was issued after these talks. When Khrushchev left Peking Oct. 4, Mao did not come out to the airport to see him off.

According to a 1963 issue of Communist China's *Peking Review*, Khrushchev tried during this visit to persuade the Chinese to tone down their campaign to liberate Taiwan. The question of Taiwan was an "incendiary factor" that created an atmosphere of imminent war, Khrushchev was said to have contended. The Chinese rejected Khrushchev's view as "absurd." They were said to suspect that Khrushchev was in league with Eisenhower in trying to impose Washington's "2 Chinas" policy on China.

Before returning to Moscow Oct. 10, Khrushchev, at a meeting in Novosibirsk Oct. 9 (his speech was made public in Moscow Oct. 13), reiterated "that the search for peaceful coexistence was "the root question of our time." He said: His "talks in America showed that the majority of the American people do not want war and are striving. . .[for] peaceful cooperation"; "coexistence means continuation of the struggle between the 2 social systems—but by peaceful means, without war, without interference by one state in the internal affairs of another"; "we consider it to be [an] economic, political and ideological struggle, but not military."

U.S. Response to Sino-Soviet Rift

The U.S. government apparently was aware of the rift then growing between the Soviet Union and Communist China. State Secy. Christian Herter commented at his news conference Oct. 6 that the USSR and Communist China each seemed to follow "a rather different line" on the solution of international disputes by negotiation instead of by force. He noted that while Khrushchev, during his China visit, had "talked quite eloquently" on the need for a peaceful East-West settlement, Mao Tse-tung "never made any statement" on the subject, "either on Mr. Khrushchev's arrival or. . .departure."

Nonetheless, Herter declared: "There is no question in our minds that [the USSR's] demand for recognition as the leader of the Communist world places upon the Russians a degree of responsibility for the actions of other members of the bloc that is very real." He made it clear that this responsibility specifically applied to Communist China's actions with respect to Laos, Korea and Taiwan. Herter said that it was "very difficult" to tell just how "deep" were "the differences" between Moscow and Peking but that by all "outward appearances" the 2 Communist powers were still "working very closely together."

The State Department singled out Communist China for intensified criticism. State Undersecy. C. Douglas Dillon denounced the Peking government Oct. 7 for its refusal to accept Khrushchev's proposal on the renunciation of force. Recalling the unyielding attitude shown by the Communist Chinese ambassador at the Warsaw talks, Dillon said: "The Peiping régime has demonstrated absolutely no disposition to make the slightest move toward an agreement on a cease-fire or a renunciation of force. Its recalcitrance at the negotiating table has been maintained since the talks were resumed in Warsaw more than a full year ago."

Communist China was denounced by Assistant State Secy. Andrew H. Berding (for Public Affairs) Oct. 16 as the greatest threat to world peace in light of the "improvement in the international atmosphere" created by the Eisenhower-Khrushchev talks. Addressing the National Association of Broadcasters in Washington, Berding said that the Eisenhower-Khrushchev accords had not produced "any significant promise of relaxation of tensions in the Far East." He said: "Either Peiping. . . does not share Moscow's professed desire for a relaxation of tensions or Peiping does not regard such professions as genuine." Berding welcomed Khrushchev's earlier advice to Chinese Communist leaders not to "test" the capitalist system by force or to attempt to impose "socialism by force of arms." But he said: "We believe that if the Soviet Union is sincere in wanting to safeguard the peace, it has the leverage. . . to insure a measure of responsibility on the part of the Chinese Communists."

U.S. Amb.-to-UN Lodge called on the UN Oct. 20 to condemn Communist China for the "crime of" violating Tibet's basic rights and for genocide against the Tibetan people. He denounced as "specious arguments" the proposals of Britain and France to treat Tibet as an "internal" Chinese matter outside of UN competence. Ridiculing Soviet opposition to UN action on Tibet, Lodge said the UN had been "asked to believe that it is all right for Chinese Communists to kill Tibetans but that it is a provocation for us to talk about it."

Sino-Indian Border Dispute

In late Oct. 1959 a serious border incident involved Indian police and Chinese "frontier guards" 100 miles east of Leh, the capital of the Ladakh district in eastern Kashmir. The Indian External Affairs Ministry reported Oct. 23 that Chinese Communists had attacked an Indian border patrol and killed at least 17 men in the remote Kashmirian section. Indian Prime Min. Jawaharlal Nehru said Oct. 24 that the area of the clash was "part of India" and asserted that Indians would "defend our territory and our prestige and our honor."

Peking's version was quite different. A Communist Chinese note to the Indian government Oct. 23 maintained that Indian troops had fired on Chinese soldiers located "within China's administrative jurisdiction." Peking Oct. 26 issued a Foreign Ministry statement in which Communist China laid claim to more than 6,000 square miles of the district.

The statement, made public Oct. 30 by the Chinese embassy in New Delhi asserted that the disputed section of Ladakh "has always been under China's administrative jurisdiction." It cited as evidence a road that had been built across Ladakh by China in 1957 and had been used "without hindrance." The statement said that the "customary boundary" between China and Ladakh extended south from Karakoram Pass through Kongka Pass to the southwest, then south across the western part of Lake Pangkong. It warned that if armed Indians insisted on patrolling this area, Chinese forces "would have all the more reason" to enter northeastern India. (The border claimed by Communist China passed 70 miles east of Leh. The traditional Indian border was located 140 miles east of Leh.)

Indian sources reported Oct. 30 that the version of the Chinese statement delivered to India had indicated that Communist China would recognize the McMahon Line as the Indian-Tibetan frontier if India recognized Chinese claims in Ladakh. The statement made public by the Chinese embassy conceded that the disputed area south of the McMahon Line had not been under Chinese jurisdiction for some time and that China sought adjustment of the 700-mile Tibet-India border through "negotiations."

Soviet Premier Nikita S. Khrushchev told the Supreme Soviet (Russian parliament) in Moscow Oct. 31 that he "would be happy if there were no more incidents on the Sino-Indian frontier and if the . ∴. Sino-Indian disputes were settled by. . . friendly negotiations. Khrushchev said he was "especially sorry about these incidents causing casualties to both sides." He balanced his "regret" over the incident by repeating Soviet support for Peking's professed rôle as a major power and for its claims to Taiwan.

Speaking before a Congress Party rally in New Delhi Nov. 1, Prime Min. Nehru said that India was making "adequate military preparations" to meet Communist Chinese "aggression" against India's frontiers. Nehru told Indians that they "should not be afraid just because China is a big nation." "Our country is not a small nation either," he said. Nehru had been under attack by Indian newspapers and political leaders for his failure to act against the Communist Chinese incursions. He declared: "We have no intention of attacking any nation, nor are we prepared to tolerate any attack on us."

Nehru said Nov. 5 that the Sino-Indian border dispute was not the sort to precipitate a "real war" but that India was prepared to take whatever "strong action" was necessary in defense of India's territorial integrity. Nehru asserted that he could not "conceive of any power on earth that" would "make me surrender."

Communist Chinese Premier Chou En-lai proposed in a letter to Nehru Nov. 7 that the 2 heads of government meet to discuss the boundary dispute. Chou also proposed that both sides withdraw their armed forces "20 kilometers [12½ miles]... from the so-called McMahon Line in the east and from the line up to which each side exercises actual control in the west [the Ladakh district of Kashmir]." (The Chinese followed up this proposal Nov. 14 by releasing 10 captured Indians and returning the bodies of 9 slain Indian policemen.) Under the buffer proposal, Chinese troops would evacuate a 12½-mile-wide strip of border territory but would retain most Indian-claimed territory they occupied.

A Nehru memo to Indian diplomats abroad, reported Nov. 11 by the *N.Y. Times*, expressed doubt that China would abandon its claims to Indian territory. It said India would have no alternative but to reoccupy forcibly the disputed area when weather permitted.

(The Indian Communist Party National Council, meeting

Nov. 14 in Meerut, reversed its previous support of Communist China in the border dispute and declared that India had taken the "correct stand" in rejecting Peking's border claims. It urged maintenance of the *status quo* pending a negotiated settlement of the conflict.)

Nehru refused Nov. 16 to meet with Chou En-lai until "preliminary steps" had been taken toward an "interim understanding" on the conflicting border claims. Nehru told the Indian parliament that a new Indian note had rejected China's proposal for a mutual withdrawal of troops from a border buffer zone as "impracticable."

Nehru Nov. 20 read to the Indian parliament a note in which he had proposed to Peking that both countries pull back all their forces from the disputed areas before any negotiations began. He called his offer "an interim measure to avoid border clashes" and repeated his stand that the area in dispute "has been for long years part of India." Nehru was quoted in the *Christian Science Monitor* Nov. 22 as having suggested that the incident had been caused by the seemingly Stalinist views prevailing in Chinese foreign policy and by Communist China's apparent inability to understand the world outside its borders.

Washington at first took a neutral stance. U.S. State Secy. Herter, while reaffirming the U.S.' sympathy for India, told newsmen Nov. 12 that the Indian-Chinese-Tibetan border was "ill-defined" and that the U.S. lacked "first-hand knowledge, particularly. . .[about] the northwestern area, with respect to the definitive border that could rightly be claimed by either side." He said the U.S. "presume[d] that the claims made by the Indians" were "valid claims" but that the U.S. had "only the word of a friend [India]" to corroborate them.

In a clarification issued later Nov. 12, after Indian and U.S. sources had criticized his failure to back India, Herter condemned Communist China's use of force in the dispute and explained that he had dealt only with the "legalities" of the problem.

In a statement made to Indian Chargé d'Affaires D. N. Chatterjee Nov. 13, Herter apologized for "any possible misconceptions" of his position on the dispute. He made clear that his remarks "were not meant to imply any condonement by the [U.S.] government of the use of force by the Chinese Communists." He said that the U.S. "strongly sympathizes with India's attempts to resolve the present issues with Communist China peacefully."

In India, Acharya J. B. Kripalani, leader of the Praja (People's) Socialist Party, charged the Nehru government Nov. 25 with "culpable negligence" in dealing with the Chinese menace. Indian Defense Min. V. K. Krishna Menon defended himself before parliament Nov. 26 against charges that he had failed to take military action to oppose Chinese incursions in northern India. Conceding that India's "policy was not to deploy troops" before its frontiers were threatened, he asserted that "the necessary troop movements consistent with our resources have taken place." He said that India was not prevented from "getting defense materials from...East or West, but we would like to pay for it" rather than accept politically conditional foreign military aid.

Defending his policies before parliament Nov. 25, Nehru had appealed for national unity behind India's neutralist aims but had warned China that "if war is thrust upon us, we shall fight with all our strength."

The Indian parliament Nov. 27 indorsed Nehru's pledges to defend Sikkim, Bhutan and Nepal against Chinese aggression. Addressing parliament at the close of a 2½-day debate on foreign affairs, Nehru declared that any aggression against Nepal (a Himalayan state having 500-mile borders with both India and China) "would be considered by us as aggression on India." Nehru conceded that he was assuming a "grave responsibility," but he defended it as necessary "not only for wider reasons but for India's own security." His pledge supplemented accords under which India was training Nepal's armed forces and both countries were required to consult on "serious friction...with any neighboring state."

Nehru told parliament Nov. 27 that while he did not think there was "any country that cares more for peace than the Soviet Union, I doubt that there is any country that cares less for peace than China." He reiterated hopes for peaceful settlement of the border dispute but warned that if war came, "we shall become a nation in arms" in a "struggle for life and death" that would "shake Asia and shake the world."

Pres. Eisenhower Dec. 2 announced plans to make a trip to Europe, the Middle East and Asia. The purpose of the trip, he said, was to demonstrate the basic U.S. aspiration "to search out methods by which peace in the world can be assured with justice for everybody." India was included on the President's itinerary. Eisenhower took the occasion to comment on the Indian-Chinese border dispute, saying that he favored India's efforts to settle the dispute through "honest negotiation."

Chinese-U.S. Incidents

While the Sino-Indian border dispute was in progress, Communist Chinese consular officials in Bombay, India Nov. 27, 1959 seized U.S. Marine Sgt. Robert Armstrong, 34, of Martinez, Calif. and held him for 6 hours. He was released bruised but otherwise unharmed to Indian police. Armstrong, working as a clerk and guard at the U.S. consulate in Bombay, reportedly was seized near the Chinese consulate while guarding Chang Chien-yuh, Bombay representative of the Communist-owned China Import-Export Corp., who had asked for political asylum at the American consulate Nov. 26. According to U.S. versions of the incident: Chang, who had signed declarations denouncing communism and had undergone a recorded interrogation Nov. 26, changed his mind about defecting Nov. 27 and ran into the Chinese consulate with the interview tapes; Armstrong was trying to retrieve the tapes when he was seized by Chinese consular personnel.

U.S. Amb.-to-India Ellsworth Bunker protested to the Indian Foreign Ministry Nov. 28 that Armstrong's seizure was "a high-handed violation of the personal rights of a... [U.S.] citizen in a friendly country." A Communist Chinese statement broadcast Nov. 29 by Peking radio charged that Chang had been "kidnapped" by U.S. consular officials Nov. 26 but had managed to escape next day. It asserted that one of the "American kidnapers" had been seized when he pursued Chang to the Chinese consulate "knife in hand." A Chinese protest to India Nov. 30 contained the same charges.

In Mar. 1960, Communist China jailed Bishop James Edward Walsh, 69, an American Roman Catholic Maryknoll missionary serving in Shanghai. Walsh was convicted and sentenced to 20 years' imprisonment by a Shanghai people's court Mar. 18 on charges of directing espionage and counter-revolutionary activities against China by a group of Chinese Roman Catholic priests. Walsh had served in Shanghai as general secretary of the Catholic Central Bureau when the city fell to the Communists in 1949 and had remained in China under surveillance and house arrest until he was arrested in Oct. 1958. Walsh was considered the leader of Roman Catholic resistance to Communist efforts to sever Chinese priests from the Vatican and to enroll them in the Communist-sponsored China Catholics' Patriotic Association. He had refused Chinese offers of repatriation to the U.S. in 1955. Walsh and 4 other U.S. citizens also held on spy charges were the only American prisoners then remaining in Communist China.

The Chinese Hsinhua news agency reported Mar. 18 that the Rev. George Germain, ex-rector of the Catholic Aurora University in Shanghai, the Rev. Fernand Lacretelle, former Jesuit chief for Shanghai, and Archbishop Antonio Riberi, former papal nuncio in China, had been members of the Roman Catholic spy net. All 3 had left China.

The U.S. Mar. 22 protested Bishop Walsh's imprisonment as an "inexcusable act" and "one more step in the. . . persecution of religion in Communist China." A note handed to Chinese Amb.-to-Poland Wang Ping-nan by U.S. Amb.-to-Poland Jacob Beam on direct orders of State Secy. Herter denounced the charges against Walsh as "totally false" and said that the U.S. viewed his conviction with "deep revulsion."

Premier Chou En-lai Apr. 10, 1960 reiterated Communist China's policy toward the U.S. in regard to Taiwan. Speaking at the closing session of the National People's Congress in Peking, Chou said that the U.S. had seized Taiwan "by force" and was trying to create "2 Chinas" to legitimatize the island's separation from China. It was China's "sacred sovereign right" to liberate Taiwan, Chou asserted, and with that "no outsider may interfere."

Foreign Min. Chen Yi, speaking in Peking at ceremonies marking Communist China's 11th anniversary, said Oct. 1 that his government would not accept an Asian settlement based on the existence of 2 Chinas. The Chinese Foreign Ministry Sept. 13 had denounced the Warsaw meetings between U.S. Amb.-to-Poland Beam and Chinese Amb.-to-Poland Wang as senseless in view of the U.S.' refusal to negotiate "fundamental issues" and of its "scheme to create "2 Chinas.' "

Sino-Soviet Ideological Split

Meanwhile, there had been increasing indications of ideological disagreement between the Soviet Union and Communist China. In Jan. 1960, the Peking government openly rejected a Soviet proposal for general and comprehensive disarmament as a basis of negotiations. In April the Sino-Soviet ideological rift became evident with the publication in *Red Flag*, the theoretical journal of the Chinese Communist Party, of a long article entitled "Long Live Leninism." The article, published in commemoration of Lenin's 90th birthday, was a critique of "revisionism" ostensibly directed against Marshal Tito of Yugoslavia. Indirectly, it was aimed at Soviet Premier Khrushchev. Attacking what it termed "attempts of the modern revisionists to distort and carve up the teachings of Lenin," it charged that by acting as if "the peace movement is everything and the final aim is nothing," these persons were seeking a peace that "may be acceptable to the imperialists" but that would "destroy" the "revolutionary will" to socialism."

In ensuing months, the polemics exchanged between Moscow and Peking increased in bitterness and involved Communist adherents around the world. At this juncture, Premier Chou En-lai in midsummer 1960 held out another offer of détente to the U.S.—this one much more specific than his Apr. 23, 1955 overture of negotiations. The U.S. at once rejected Chou's proposal.

During a reception at the Swiss embassy in Peking Aug. 1, Chou proposed a "peace pact" between China, the U.S. and other Pacific powers to set up a "non-nuclear zone in Asia and the Western Pacific." He said that China had not "given up its policy of seeking peaceful relations with countries with different social systems." In Washington Aug. 1, State Department press officer Lincoln White said that the matter had never been broached at the Sino-American talks in Warsaw and termed Chou's offer a "propaganda gesture."

The Communist Chinese démarche was later interpreted by some observers as a studied Peking reaction to Soviet Premier Khrushchev's assertion June 21 to the 3d Rumanian Workers' (Communist) Party Congress in Bucharest that "under present conditions, war is not inevitable" and that "he who does not understand this does not believe in the. . . great attractive force of socialism, which has manifestly demonstrated its superiority over capitalism." (Peking commented in *Jenmin Jih Pao* June 29 that "only when the imperialist. . . and capitalist systems. . . are really abolished can there really be lasting world peace.")

KENNEDY-NIXON DEBATES (1960)

Kennedy Would Not Defend Quemoy & Matsu

John F. Kennedy, elected in Nov. 1960, became U.S. President Jan. 20, 1961. He inherited the Eisenhower-Dulles policy of containing Communist China. By the time he was inaugurated, these main ingredients of that policy had already been well established: the nonrecognition of Communist China, a firm opposition to a seat for Peking in the UN, an espousal of the defense of Taiwan and a readiness for prompt assistance to the countries on the periphery of China threatened by a Communist take-over.

During the 1960 Presidential election campaign, Kennedy, then the junior Senator from Massachusetts, and his opponent, U.S. Vice Pres. Richard M. Nixon, had held a series of debates before countrywide TV audiences and had taken up the issue of the U.S. policy on the defense of the offshore islands. During the 2d of these debates, Kennedy said Oct. 7 that he "believe[d] strongly in the defense of Formosa [Taiwan]" but that "if you're going to get into war for the defense of Formosa, it ought to be on a clearly defined line." "I do not believe that that line in case of a war should be drawn on those islands [Quemoy and Matsu]," Kennedy declared. "As long as they are not essential to the defense of Formosa, it's been my judgment ever since 1954. . .that our line should be drawn in the sea around the island [Taiwan] itself." He pointed out that Quemoy and Matsu were "5 or 6 miles off the coast of Communist China, within a general harbor area and more than 100 miles from Formosa."

The U.S. "has on occasion attempted—mostly in the middle '50s—to persuade Chiang Kai-shek to pull his troops back to Formosa," Kennedy said. He recalled that when State Secy. Christian Herter was State Undersecretary in 1958, Herter had said the 2 islands "were strategically undefensible." Adm. Raymond Spruance, Gen. J. Lawton

Collins and Gen. Matthew B. Ridgway had "said that we should not attempt to defend these islands." Kennedy asserted. But "I would not suggest the withdrawal at the point of the Communist gun," Kennedy continued. "It is a decision finally that the Nationalists should make, and I believe that we should consult with them and attempt to work out a plan by which the line is drawn at the Island of Formosa." "I think it's unwise," Kennedy asserted, "to take the chance of being dragged into a war which may lead to a world war over 2 islands which are not strategically defensible. . .[or] essential to the defense of Formosa."

Nixon said he "disagree[d] completely" with Kennedy. He recalled that "immediately before the Korean War, South Korea was supposed to be indefensible. . . . Generals testified to that, and [State] Secy. [Dean] Acheson made a very famous speech. . .indicating in effect that South Korea was beyond the [U.S.'] defense zone." "As far as Quemoy and Matsu are concerned," Nixon continued, "the question is not these 2 little pieces of real estate—they are unimportant. It isn't the few people who live on them—they are not too important. It's the principle involved. These 2 islands are in the area of freedom. . . . We should not force our Nationalist allies to get off them and give them to the Communists. . . [lest] we start a chain reaction, because the Communists aren't after Quemoy and Matsu. They're after Formosa. . . . This is the same kind of woolly thinking that led to disaster for America in Korea. . . . I would never tolerate it as President. . . ."

During their 3d debate, Nixon reiterated Oct. 13 that if the Chinese Communists attacked Quemoy and Matsu as "a prelude to an attack on Formosa, which would be the indication today," the U.S. would "honor our treaty obligations and stand by our ally, Formosa." But he refused to tell how he would respond to such an attack. He said "it would be completely irresponsible" for a President or Presidential candidate "to indicate the course of action and the weapons

he would use." Nixon said: "To do what Sen. Kennedy has
suggested, to suggest that we will surrender these islands or
force our Chinese Nationalist allies to surrender them in
advance," would lead "to war." The Chinese Communists
"don't want just Quemoy and Matsu" or "just Formosa."
"They want the world," and "if you. . .indicate in advance
that you're not going to defend any part of the free world. . . ,
it doesn't satisfy them. It only whets their appetite, and then
. . . when do you stop them?"

Kennedy replied: The U.S. had agreed, in the U.S.-
Nationalist Chinese treaty "which I voted for. . .in 1955, to
defend Formosa and the Pescadores islands." Sen. Theodore
F. Green (D., R.I.) had received from Pres. Eisenhower
Oct. 2, 1958 a letter promising that "neither you nor any
other American need feel the United States will be involved
in military hostilities merely in the defense of Quemoy and
Matsu." Eisenhower's letter stated "the present American
position." "The treaty does not include these 2 islands.
Mr. Nixon suggests that the United States should go to war
if those 2 islands are attacked. I suggest that if Formosa is
attacked, or the Pescadores, or if there is any military action
in any area which indicates an attack on Formosa and the
Pescadores, then, of course, the United States is at war to
defend its treaty." Nixon apparently "wants us to be committed to the defense of these islands as free territory, not
as part of the defense of Formosa."

Kennedy quoted the late Adm. Harry E. Yarnell, pre-
World War II commander of the U.S. Asiatic Fleet, as
saying that "these islands are not worth the bones of a
single American."

Kennedy asked why Nixon had taken "a different position" from (1) Eisenhower, who "never advocated that
Quemoy and Matsu should be defended under all circumstances as a matter of principle," and (2) the late John
Foster Dulles, who had said at a 1958 press conference that
he thought it "a mistake for Chiang Kai-shek to deploy

troops to these islands." Nixon replied that (a) "the implica-
tion...of everything" Dulles had said at the 1958 press
conference was that "when the troops were withdrawn...
Quemoy could better be defended" and (b) Eisenhower
"had always indicated" that in dealing with dictators, "we
must not make the mistake...of indicating that we are
going to make a concession at the point of a gun" because
"inevitably the dictator is encouraged to try it again."

Nixon said he thought "the Senate was right" when, with
Sen. Lyndon B. Johnson and "a majority of the Democrats,"
it "rejected Sen. Kennedy's position in 1955" by a 70–12
vote. "We're not going to have peace by giving in and indicating in advance that we are not going to defend what
had become a symbol of freedom," Nixon asserted.

Kennedy replied: "I don't think it's possible for Mr.
Nixon to state the record in distortion of the facts with
more precision than he just did." Dulles, at a 1955 press
conference, had said that the U.S.-Nationalist Chinese
treaty "excludes Quemoy and Matsu from the treaty area.
That was done with much thought and deliberation.... I
completely sustained the treaty. I voted for it. I would take
any action necessary to defend the treaty, Formosa and the
Pescadore Islands.... I would not hand over these islands
under any point of gun. But...the treaty is quite precise,
and I sustain the treaty. Mr. Nixon would add a guarantee
to islands 5 miles off the [Chinese] coast...when he's never
really protested the Communists' seizing Cuba 90 miles off
the [U.S.] coast."

White House Press Secy. James C. Hagerty told reporters
Oct. 15, 1960 that Nixon and Pres. Eisenhower had con-
ferred by phone Oct. 14 and found themselves in agreement
on U.S. policy toward the defense of Quemoy and Matsu.
Their positions were "exactly as stated in the letter the
President sent to Sen. [Theodore F.] Green on Oct. 5, 1958,"
Hagerty said.

Kennedy asserted in a statement issued in Washington Oct. 15 that Nixon "has now retreated to the Administration's view on Quemoy-Matsu, as contained in the 1955 treaty and resolution, which I have supported ever since. . . . Mr. Nixon had previously implied that he wishes to extend our commitment to defend these 2 islands against all attacks regardless of whether the attack was part of a general attack on Formosa. This, in my opinion, would have. . . increased the possibilities of military danger."

Kennedy suggested in a "Meet the Press" TV interview in Washington Oct. 16 that the Quemoy-Matsu dispute should be ended because, he said, Nixon had joined him in backing the Administration position rather than supporting the "entirely different position" Nixon had taken previously. Kennedy said he opposed "endanger[ing] the security of the United States" by letting the Chinese Communists "think we are divided."

CHINA ISOLATED (1961-3)

Peking Retreats from the 'Great Leap'

The inauguration of the Democratic Administration in Washington coincided in time with a major shift in Communist China's domestic policy. Communist China's campaign for a "great leap forward" in industry, begun in 1958, was ordered curtailed Jan. 20, 1961 in favor of increased stimulation of larger farm output. The decision was reached in Peking at a meeting Jan. 14–18 of the Chinese Communist Party Central Committee, presided over by Party Chairman Mao Tse-t'ing, and was made public in a communiqué issued Jan. 20 through the Hsinhua News Agency.

The communiqué, adopted Jan. 18, admitted that China's grain production had fallen short of the 297 million tons planned for 1960. It blamed the failure on "the most severe natural calamities in a century following upon the serious natural calamities of 1959." Confirming recurrent reports of food shortages approaching famine in some areas, the communiqué warned that "the temporary difficulties in supplying the market caused by the poor harvest and the shortage of raw materials for light industry are important problems" needing quick solution. "Inasmuch as tremendous [industrial] development had been achieved over the last 3 years," the statement declared, ". . . the scope of capital construction should be appropriately reduced." It ordered "prompt steps to help the development of light industry. . .and suburban agriculture, . . . consumer goods" and non-staple food.

The communiqué asserted that some of the difficulties were due to "sabotage" by "bad elements" in the Communist Party, "landlord, bourgeois and other elements seduced by reactionaries." It charged that these groups had "made use of the difficult conditions created by natural disasters and certain defects." It ordered the immediate

143

start of a purge "throughout the country . . . , area by area," to "clear the party of [bad] elements that infiltrated into the party and government departments."

The communiqué also announced orders for a reduction in the work hours and the elimination of some of the strict work controls imposed on commune workers. (The *N.Y. Times* reported Jan. 29 that communal production brigades had received fuller freedom in the use of their manpower and machinery and that farmers would be paid on a basis of brigade, rather than commune, production and income. It reported Feb. 1 that the shift in the control of farm work was leading to a dissolution of the commune system and its replacement by production brigades formed by relatively small numbers of farm families. The right to small private plots and restricted numbers of private livestock was said to have been restored.)

The communiqué reported the approval of the world-policy statement issued Dec. 1960 at a meeting in Moscow of 81 Communist parties. It denounced "United States imperialism" as the chief danger to the world and asserted that "the most pressing task now is to prevent the engineering of a new war by the imperialists." (These sections were deleted from a version of the communiqué published Jan. 26 by the Soviet Communist Party newspaper *Pravda*, purportedly as the full text.)

A declaration published Jan. 21 by the Chinese Communist Party Central Committee at the end of a plenary meeting in Peking accepted Soviet views that war was not inevitable. It labeled the U.S. as the "main enemy of the peoples of the whole world." The Chinese declaration affirmed that "a new world war can be prevented by the joint efforts of the powerful forces of our era—the Socialist camp, the . . . working class, the national liberation movement. . . ." It repeated its acceptance of the Soviet thesis that "revolution is the affair of the peoples in various countries" and that Communists opposed "the export of revolution." It said, however, that "they also oppose the imperialist export of counterrevolution" and "imperialist interference in the internal affairs of people. . . who have risen in revolution."

Premier Chou En-lai, in an interview given U.S. newsman Edgar Snow in 1960 (copyrighted by Snow and published in the Jan. 31, 1961 issue of *Look*), conceded that the USSR and Communist China differed on many matters but not in their views on foreign policy, especially on the non-inevitability of war. Chou said China supported Russia's proposals for general disarmament and peaceful coexistence and would work to implement them despite its exclusion from the UN. He said, however, that China would not be bound by any disarmament agreement reached without its participation. He expressed the belief that a U.S.-Chinese settlement would be achieved, but not before U.S. troops were withdrawn from Taiwan and the U.S. accepted Communist Chinese views that Taiwan was a domestic Chinese problem.

Nonrecognition Policy Continued

The changes in Washington and Peking did not produce any significant change in the U.S.-Communist Chinese relations. Pres. Kennedy Jan. 25, 1961 discouraged the suggestion that the U.S. offer Communist China food to alleviate famine. He said at a news conference that he was "not anxious to offer food if it's regarded merely as a propaganda effort." He noted that Communist China had recently exported quantities of food and said that in view of the Chinese' "belligerent attitude," there was "no indication. . . that they would respond favorably" to U.S. aid.

The U.S. State Department announced Jan. 28 that it had asked for a postponement of U.S.-Communist Chinese negotiations on the release of U.S. citizens held by China. Kennedy indicated to newsmen Feb. 1 that the talks, carried on by the U.S. and Chinese ambassadors in Warsaw, had been delayed to study a fresh approach on the matter. He warned that "as long as these men are held, it will be extremely difficult to have any kind of normal relations" with Communist China.

The new Administration's China policy was outlined by the new U.S. State Secretary, Dean Rusk, at a news conference Feb. 6. Rusk reaffirmed the U.S. commitment to defend Taiwan. He said: The U.S. had "strong commitments to our ally," Nationalist China. "That commitment is firm" despite Communist China's view that it was "a major obstacle" to a settlement with the U.S. The question of Chinese representation in the UN was conditioned by "the highly complicated parliamentary situation" in the UN. The U.S. was studying proposals for including Communist China in world disarmament negotiations; "it will not be easy to achieve any realistic or effective disarmament unless all those countries that are capable of producing...large armed forces are brought within the system."

Britain and the U.S. continued to differ in their approaches to China. The Anglo-U.S. disagreement on recognizing Communist China and admitting it to the UN was revived Feb. 8 when the Earl of Home, British foreign secretary, told the House of Lords that "the facts of international life require that Communist China should be seated" in the UN.

Home conceded that Communist China had "few of the credentials of a peace-loving country." He denounced the Peking régime for "smothering" Tibet, rejecting all efforts at conciliation and proclaiming its belief—Home said—in the inevitability of a new world war. He made it clear, however, that Britain viewed Communist China's entry into the UN as essential if it were to be brought back into the international community. He said that the USSR bore its share of the blame as well for tensions in the newly emerging states and asserted that it was for "Khrushchev to say if he is going to use the Laotians, the Congolese and the Cubans

as pawns in the cold war or whether he is going to open. . .
real coexistence."

The U.S. State Department immediately dissociated
itself from the position taken by Home. A U.S. disavowal of
any connection with the British view was issued Feb. 9 in a
State Department statement that said there had been no
prior consultation between Britain and the U.S. on the
subject. State Secy. Dean Rusk said at a Washington news
conference Mar. 9 that Communist China itself had adopted
a position that would preclude its admission to the UN unless
Nationalist Chinese representatives were unseated. He expressed doubt that this could be done without creating "a
very serious problem" for the UN's future.

Pres. Kennedy said at his news conference Mar. 8 that
his Administration's first effort to negotiate an improvement
of U.S.-Chinese relations had been rejected by Peking.
Kennedy said that Communist China had shown itself to
be "extremely belligerent toward us" and that perhaps this
was due to Peking's recognition of U.S. commitments "to
maintaining its connections with other countries," presumably Nationalist China. He made it clear that the U.S. was
"not prepared to surrender" to attain a relaxation of tensions
with mainland China.

The President's statement referred to the resumption in
Warsaw Mar. 7 of the diplomatic-level talks between U.S.
Amb.-to-Poland Jacob D. Beam and Chinese Amb. Wang
Ping-nan. State Department spokesmen reported Mar. 8
that Beam had requested negotiations on an exchange of
news correspondents, the release of Americans held by Communist China and a pledge for the peaceful settlement of
U.S.-Chinese differences. Wang reportedly had refused negotiation of any of these matters until the U.S. pledged to
withdraw its forces from Taiwan.

A Communist Chinese Foreign Ministry statement
broadcast Mar. 13 denied responsibility for the failure to

begin negotiations on the U.S. proposals. It declared that the stationing of U.S. troops on Taiwan was proof of American hostility toward China.

Outside the Administration, the American public was, as before, divided on U.S. policy toward Communist China. The Committee of One Million, a private U.S. group formed to oppose Chinese admission to the UN, announced Feb. 19 that 54 Senators and 285 Representatives had indorsed a committee restatement of its views. Harold E. Stassen, ex-U.S. disarmament aide, disclosed Feb. 14 that he had written Pres. Kennedy to advocate that the U.S. support UN admission for Communist China and East and West Germany. Sens. Wayne Morse (D., Ore.) and George D. Aiken (R., Vt.) predicted Feb. 16 that the UN votes of newly independent African states would make Red China's admission likely at the UN Assembly's 16th session.

John K. Galbraith, who had been designated to be U.S. ambassador to India, told the Senate Foreign Relations Committee Mar. 24 that U.S. recognition and UN admission of Communist China was necessary to insure peace in Asia but that neither was possible until China renounced its aggressive policies and accepted the existence of the Nationalist Chinese régime on Taiwan. Supreme Court Justice William O. Douglas said Apr. 5 that although Communist China was aggressive and expansionist, the U.S. could no longer afford to ignore its existence and block its UN entry.

The Senate June 28 adopted by 76–0 vote and sent to the House a resolution opposing UN membership for or U.S. recognition of Communist China. The resolution was approved after a renewed month-long GOP drive against any shift in U.S. policy on the issue. Republican anxiety had been revived as a result of reports (denied by State Secy. Rusk in Chicago June 27) that the Kennedy Administration was considering a plan to propose that both Chinas get equal UN General Assembly representation.

The Kennedy Administration explored plans to establish diplomatic relations with Outer Mongolia, a Communist régime that the Nationalist Chinese had consistently rejected and ignored. These reported plans were attacked July 13, 1961 by Republican leaders Everett M. Dirksen (Ill.) of the Senate and Charles A. Halleck (Ind.) of the House. Chairman Styles Bridges (N.H.) of the Senate Republican Policy Committee demanded July 25 that the U.S. reject any "package deal" under which the U.S. would recognize Outer Mongolia and the USSR would withhold its veto of UN membership for Mauritania. Bridges warned that "we always seem to come out losers" on deals with the USSR and that the "recognition of Outer Mongolia would merely be a side-door device to make the recognition of Red China a bit easier to put over at an early date."

Confronted with such opposition from Congress, the State Department announced Aug. 11 that the U.S. was suspending its "exploration" of plans to establish diplomatic relations with Outer Mongolia.

Kennedy's decision not to recognize Outer Mongolia yet, it was reported, was part of a plan for keeping Communist China out of the UN and Nationalist China in. This plan was said to be based on a supposition that if the U.S. mollified Nationalist China by rejecting Mongolian relations, the U.S. might more easily persuade Nationalist China not to block UN membership for Outer Mongolia. The USSR, therefore, would have no cause to fulfill its threat of matching a Nationalist Chinese veto of UN membership for Outer Mongolia with a Soviet veto of UN membership for Mauritania. Some U.S. diplomats had said that African UN delegations— especially those of the French community—would be angry at Nationalist China for causing such a Soviet veto of Mauritania and, therefore, might vote against Nationalist China on the issue of a UN seat for Communist China.

A U.S. pledge to back Nationalist China's continued

UN membership and to oppose UN membership for Communist China was given by Kennedy during conferences at the White House July 31–Aug. 1 with Gen. Chen Cheng, 63, Nationalist China's vice president and premier. Nationalist Chinese Foreign Min. Shen Chang-huan, U.S. State Secy. Rusk and other U.S. and Chinese officials participated in the talks, whose subject matter ranged from Berlin to foreign aid. Chen and his party had arrived in the U.S. for a 10-day visit July 30. His invitation had been tendered on Kennedy's initiative.

In a joint communiqué issued Aug. 2, Kennedy and Cheng said they had exchanged views on the UN membership applications of Outer Mongolia and Mauritania and had expressed "concern" at the Soviet veto of membership for Mauritania. According to press sources, Kennedy had been unable to persuade the Chinese Nationalists not to veto UN membership for Outer Mongolia. Chen had reiterated in a National Press Club talk Aug. 1 that Nationalist China would use every power available to it in the UN to block Outer Mongolian membership. Since the USSR had warned that it would continue to veto Mauritania's entry as long as Nationalist China barred Outer Mongolia, the U.S. conferees told the Chinese that some UN delegations—especially new ones from Africa—might blame Nationalist China for the veto of Mauritania and consequently might swing to the Chinese Communists in the dispute over which of the 2 Chinas deserved a UN seat.)

The communiqué said that the U.S. intended to continue military and economic aid to Taiwan.

Both Mauritania and Outer Mongolia were admitted to the UN Oct. 27, 1961 during the 16th session of the General Assembly. Nationalist China refrained from using its veto to block the admission of Outer Mongolia.

For the first time since 1950, the UN General Assembly also debated—at its 16th session—the question of Communist China's representation in the UN. Previously, the matter had been considered by the Assembly's steering committee but had been deferred. The U.S. had announced at the start of the 16th session that it would not oppose Assembly debate of Communist Chinese representation.

The debate on Communist Chinese representation was begun by the Assembly Dec. 1. Leading the opposition to Communist China's admission, U.S. Amb.-to-UN Adlai E. Stevenson denounced the Peking government for aggression in Korea, Tibet and Vietnam and warned that "the whole future of the United Nations may be at stake" unless the Assembly rejected the Soviet admission proposal. Replying to Stevenson's charges that mainland China had threatened aggression against the Nationalist régime, Soviet Rep.-to-UN Valerian Zorin said it was Communist China's own business whether it used force or other means for the "liquidation of the Chiang Kai-shek clique."

Zorin led Soviet bloc delegates in a walkout from the Assembly Dec. 1 when Nationalist delegate Tingfu F. Tsiang denounced Communist China's leaders as "even more bellicose than their Russian comrades, if that is possible." Zorin had termed the Nationalist government "a rotten political corpse" kept "alive by sops from the master's table."

The U.S. won Assembly indorsement Dec. 15, by 61–34 vote (7 abstentions), of a resolution making any substantive resolution dealing with Chinese representation subject to approval by a ⅔ majority.

The Assembly then voted Dec. 15, by 48 to 37 (19 abstentions), to reject the Soviet draft resolution calling for Nationalist China's expulsion from the UN and its replacement by Communist China.

The majority against Communist Chinese representation was composed of the U.S. and most of its West European allies, all Latin American states except Cuba, France and several former French African nations, Nationalist China and the SEATO powers, and Canada and several Commonwealth nations. Voting with the USSR and Soviet bloc in favor of Communist Chinese representation were Britain, Denmark, Norway, Sweden, Cuba, India and several neutralist states and Ghana, Guinea and several newly independent African nations. British Rep.-to-UN Joseph B. Godber told the Assembly Dec. 15 that Britain had voted for the resolution because it believed that Communist China should be in the UN but that Britain would not support Security Council action needed to expel Nationalist China.

Tacit Sino-U.S. Cooperation on Laos

Laos' neutrality and independence were guaranteed July 23, 1962 after 14 months of off-and-on negotiations in Geneva by the U.S., Communist China, the Soviet Union, France, Britain, Laos and 8 other countries. A word from Peking to Washington via Warsaw early in May 1961 had paved the way for the Geneva talks.

During Kennedy's first year as President, the crisis in Laos had received much of his personal attention. The country was in a 3-sided civil war. The paratrooper Capt. Kong Le had staged a coup against the right-wing government of Premier Tiao Samsonith in Aug. 1960 and had brought back into office the neutralist premier, Prince Souvanna Phouma. A rival government led by Prince Boun Oum was set up in Svannakhet in Sept. 1960 under the aegis of the Royal Laotian Army led by Gen. Phoumi Nosavan, who retook Vientiane in December. Souvanna Phouma fled to Cambodia, and Kong Le's force joined up with the Pathet Lao. The Soviet Union began airlifting supplies to the rebel Pathet Lao-neutralist forces.

According to Theodore C. Sorensen, a former Kennedy aide, Pres. Eisenhower in his talks with Pres.-elect Kennedy Jan. 19, 1961 had called the Laotian situation "the most immediately dangerous 'mess'." "You might have to go in there and fight it out," Sorensen quoted Eisenhower as telling Kennedy.

But Kennedy reversed the Eisenhower policy of assisting the anti-Communist right-wing force in Laos. He said at his first presidential news conference that he hoped for the establishment of Laos as "a peaceful country—an independent country not dominated by either side."

King Svang Vathana of Laos Feb. 19, 1961 proclaimed the nonalignment policy of his country (in a statement drawn up by the U.S. State Department). He appealed to Cambodia, Burma and Malaya to form a commission that would help restore peace in Laos and ensure its neutrality. Cambodia rejected the proposal despite an appeal for its acceptance by Kennedy in a reported personal message to Prince Norodom Sihanouk, Cambodian chief of state. Norodom, answering Kennedy's note Feb. 25, was said to have held that the proposed 3-power commission could not succeed unless it were able to operate in all areas of Laos. The rejection of the plan by the Pathet Lao and Souvanna Phouma's rebel government-in-exile meant that the proposed commission could not function in rebel-held northern Laos, Norodom declared.

Burmese Premier U Nu also rejected the proposal Feb. 25 on the ground that it would require Burmese recognition of the right-wing Premier Boun Oum's government. Nu said Burma had refused to recognize either of the 2 rival Laotian régimes. The Malayan government was reported Feb. 25 to favor the 3-power commission but, in the absence of other support, it declined to agree to participate.

Souvanna Phouma landed in a rebel-held area of Laos' Plaine des Jarres Feb. 22 for his first visit to Laos since the collapse of his neutralist government in 1960. Souvanna, who had permitted the formation of a provisional cabinet in his name in rebel-held northern Laos, previously had resisted demands for his personal presence among the rebels. The *N.Y. Times* reported Mar. 1 from Phongsavan, provisional Pathet Lao capital in Xiengkhouang Province (northern Laos), that Souvanna had met with Prince Souphanouvong, his half-brother and leader of the Pathet Lao, during his visit.

In a statement issued after a meeting with his cabinet in Phongsavan Feb. 25, Souvanna said his government had "recognized all areas liberated by the [rebel] army" and planned to extend its authority into other areas. A declaration made public in Pnompenh Mar. 2, after Souvanna's return to Cambodia, called for: (1) creation of a coalition government including the Pathet Lao and the withdrawal of U.S. personnel from Laos; (2) the formation of "an entirely neutral, nonpolitical government"; and (3) the convening of a 14-nation conference on Laos to set up a commission to supervise the election of a new Laotian régime.

The *N.Y. Times* reported Mar. 3 that massive shipments of Soviet arms accompanied by North Vietnamese military advisors were on the way to the Pathet Lao rebels. The *Times* dispatch, filed Mar. 1 from Phongsavan, reported that arms, including heavy artillery, armored cars, machineguns and munitions, were arriving in the capital weekly in convoys of Soviet-built trucks from Vinh, North Vietnam. An additional 45 tons of arms and supplies were said to be arriving in Xiengkhouang daily via a Soviet airlift from North Vietnam. Rebel paratroop units commanded by Capt. Kong Le were said to have been replaced on all key fronts by regular Pathet Lao forces. All leftist forces, both paratroop and Pathet Lao units, were said to be commanded by Col. Sinkapo, the Pathet Lao military commander. North Vietnamese technicians were said to be actively aiding the rebel forces.

The U.S. State Department charged Mar. 3 that the report proved that the USSR was "stalling the efforts to reach a genuine settlement while they move in more arms and solidify Communist control over the northern half of Laos."

An agreement in principle on joint efforts to restore peace and neutrality in Laos was reached in Pnompenh

Mar. 9–10 by Souvanna and Phoumi Nosavan, representing the Boun Oum government. A joint communiqué issued after their meeting declared their full agreement that: (1) "a policy of strict neutrality and a neutralization of the country by treaty are fundamental bases to restore peace and national accord"; (2) "foreign interferences must cease to allow the restoration...of mutual confidence for national reconciliation"; (3) envoys of the Boun Oum government, Souvanna's neutralist régime and the Pathet Lao rebels would meet in Pnompenh to negotiate peace after the cessation of foreign intervention; (4) a Cambodian-Malayan-Burmese commission could aid in the ending of foreign intervention in Laos.

The communiqué, approved by the Boun Oum cabinet in Vientiane Mar. 13, affirmed Phoumi's confidence in Souvanna as "the only Laotian statesman" capable of carrying out negotiations between the rightist government and Pathet Lao. It expressed support for a new 14-nation Geneva conference to arrange a final Laotian peace. The 8 other countries suggested as conference participants: Burma, Cambodia, Canada, India, North Vietnam, Poland, South Vietnam and Thailand.

Pres. Kennedy insisted on a cease-fire before negotiations toward establishing a neutral Laos. He said at his news conference Mar. 15 that "a small minority" of Laotians backed by outsiders was trying to prevent the "establishment of a neutral Laos." "We are determined to support the government and the people of Laos in resisting their attempts," Kennedy declared. To back up his statement, Kennedy ordered the 7th Fleet to the South China Sea and sent 500 marines to Thailand.

Kennedy communicated his view to the Soviet government through channels that included British Prime Min. Harold Macmillan, Indian Prime Min. Jawaharlal Nehru, U.S. Amb.-to-USSR Llwellyn Thompson and direct talks with Soviet Foreign Min. Andrei Gromyko. Kennedy's wishes for the genuine neutrality of Laos were also communicated to the Peking government in Mar. 1961 through the ambassadorial talks in Warsaw. Communist Chinese Amb.-to-Poland Wang Ping-nan was said to have responded a few months later by conveying to U.S. Amb.-to-Poland Jacob D. Beam Peking's willingness to negotiate a settlement for the neutralization of Laos.

Kenneth T. Young, former U.S. ambassador to Thailand, wrote later: "Since uncertainty over Peking's sincerity and intentions was a critical factor for Washington in determining its strategy regarding the Laotian question in 1961, Peking's notification at the ambassadorial talks in Warsaw helped to permit Washington to participate, on its part, in the difficult negotiations at Geneva."

The Geneva conference on Laos lasted from mid-May 1961 to late July 1962. The U.S. delegation, headed by W. Averell Harriman, had very few contacts with the Chinese delegation; negotiations were conducted through 3d parties, the British and Russian delegates. A coalition government was established in Vientiane June 12, 1962 with Souvanna Phouma as premier. The Declaration on the Neutrality of Laos was signed by the delegates of the 14 nations July 23. Among the signers were U.S. State Secy. Dean Rusk, Communist Chinese Foreign Min. Chen Yi and Soviet Foreign Min. Andrei Gromyko.

U.S. Escalation in Vietnam

In the meantime, the Communist guerrilla offensive in South Vietnam had led to indications of a U.S. military intervention and to an Asian fact-finding mission by Vice Pres. Lyndon B. Johnson in May 1961.

State Secy. Rusk asserted at a Washington news conference May 4 that Communist forces in South Vietnam had grown to 12,000 men and had killed or kidnapped more than 3,000 persons in 1960. Rusk declared that the U.S. would give South Vietnam "every possible help, across the entire spectrum in which help is needed," but he refused to say whether the U.S. would intervene militarily. Chairman J. William Fulbright (D., Ark.) of the Senate Foreign Relations Committee met with Pres. Kennedy later May 4 and told newsmen that he (Fulbright) would support the sending of U.S. combat troops to South Vietnam and Thailand if the Administration deemed necessary. Fulbright conceded that he had opposed U.S. military intervention in Laos, but he said that the Laotians had shown indifference to their fate whereas the South Vietnamese and Thai had proved willing to defend themselves against communism.

Kennedy announced at his news conference May 5 that Vice Pres. Johnson's trip to Asia would be a "fact-finding mission" to help the Administration decide the nature and extent of U.S. aid needed by South Vietnam. The President said: "The problem of troops...and the matter of what we are going to do to assist Vietnam obtain its independence is...still under consideration.... One of the matters which Vice Pres. Johnson will deal with [is] the problem of consultations with...Vietnam as to what further steps could most usefully be taken."

Johnson, accompanied by his wife and a party of 30 Congress members and officials, arrived in Saigon May 11. Addressing the South Vietnamese National Assembly May 12, Johnson declared that the U.S. was ready "immediately" to help expand South Vietnam's armed forces and to "meet the needs of your people on education, rural development, new industry and long-range economic development." Johnson met with Pres. Ngo Dinh Diem May 12. He said at a reception later that day that Diem was the "Churchill of today" and that the U.S. was ready to stand "shoulder to shoulder" with Vietnam in its war against communism.

Johnson flew May 13 to Manila and May 14 to Taipei, Taiwan, where he was greeted by 100,000 Chinese and began private talks with Nationalist Chinese Pres. Chiang Kai-shek. He said at a state dinner later that day: "America stands firmly with her Chinese allies [the Nationalists], and we shall continue to do so until freedom is secure." Chiang said at a news conference May 15 that Johnson had given him an unconditional pledge of continued U.S. support for Nationalist China. A joint communiqué issued by the 2 leaders later May 15 said that Johnson, "on behalf of Pres. Kennedy, assured Pres. Chiang that: the United States means to stand with her allies in the Asian area; the United States had no intention of recognizing the Peiping régime; the United States opposes seating the Peiping régime in the United Nations and regards it as important that the position of the Republic of China in the United Nations should be maintained."

Johnson returned to Washington May 24. He reported to Kennedy and then said at a press conference that the Administration would request an additional $100 million for Asian economic and military aid, the bulk to be allocated to South Vietnam, Thailand and Pakistan. (This was done in a special message sent to Congress by Kennedy May 25.) Johnson said his trip had convinced him that the U.S. must support efforts on a "broad regional basis" to "banish the curse of poverty, illness and illiteracy" in Asia. He declared that no country he visited had requested U.S. troops and that the U.S. did not plan to send armed forces to Asia.

An agreement for increased U.S. military and economic assistance for South Vietnam had been made public in the joint communiqué issued in Saigon May 13 by Johnson and Pres. Diem. The aid increases were to be used primarily (a) to strengthen the South Vietnamese civil guard and army and (b) to support social welfare and public works programs. Specific terms of the accord were negotiated in South Vietnam in June and July by a 6-member economic survey committee headed by Dr. Eugene Staley of the Stanford Research Institute. The committee's work was the subject of a report submitted to Pres. Kennedy July 29. The report urged U.S.

aid for a 15% increase in South Vietnam's armed forces, the resettlement of indefensible villages in 100 self-contained "agrovilles," and a long-range development program intended to improve the general economy and internal communications.

The Viet Cong attacks on South Vietnam had been limited to sporadic raids until May 1961. Then an apparently coordinated guerrilla offensive was launched in May against the central highlands, the southwest and Saigon area by battalion-strength units entering South Vietnam through a corridor opened for them in southern Laos by the Pathet Lao. The Viet Cong irregulars stepped up their attacks on South Vietnam near the Laotian border, and the attacks spread to other parts of South Vietnam.

Against this background, Kennedy announced at his news conference Oct. 11 that the U.S. would aid South Vietnam's defense against the intensified guerrilla campaign. He also announced his decision to send Gen. Maxwell D. Taylor to Saigon "to discuss. . .ways in which we can perhaps better assist. . .Vietnam in meeting. . .[the] threat to its independence." Responding to reporters' queries on whether he was considering sending U.S. troops to South Vietnam, Thailand or Laos, Kennedy said that "we're going to wait till Gen. Taylor comes back" with information and "then we can come to conclusions." Taylor, leaving Washington Oct. 15, said that "any American would be reluctant to use troops [in Vietnam] unless absolutely necessary."

Taylor's mission was assailed by the USSR and Communist North Vietnam on the grounds that it was a prelude to U.S. military intervention in Southeast Asia. Moscow radio political commentaries charged Oct. 12 that the Taylor mission was proof of the U.S.' "openly aggressive" plans to send troops into Vietnam. North Vietnam protested to the International Control Commission for Vietnam Oct. 14

that Taylor's visit was intended to "intensify United States intervention in South Vietnam and prepare the way for introducing United States troops" there.

Communist China's Hsinhua news agency reported Oct. 14 that North Vietnamese Pres. Ho Chi Minh had met with Communist Chinese Communist Party Chairman Mao Tse-tung and Defense Min. Lin Piao in Peking to discuss South Vietnam. Communist Chinese Premier Chou En-lai, at a Peking reception for North Vietnamese Premier Pham Van Dong, had charged June 12 that the U.S. was "preparing to embark on a war adventure in South Vietnam." Communist China, he warned, "cannot be indifferent to the increasingly grave situation caused by United States imperialism in South Vietnam."

Gen. Taylor returned to Washington Nov. 3. In his report to Pres. Kennedy, he recommended support of the South Vietnamese government of Pres. Ngo Dinh Diem, along with a limited U.S. military intervention. The U.S. Defense Department announced Feb. 8, 1962 that a new military command was being formed in South Vietnam to control all U.S. military support for the Diem government.

The new unit, the U.S. Military Assistance Command (MAC), Vietnam, was commanded by Gen. Paul D. Harkins, former U.S. Army deputy commander-in-chief in the Pacific. (Harkins, promoted from lieutenant general to full general for his new assignment, arrived in Saigon Feb. 13.) MAC, Vietnam was ordered to supervise the U.S. Military Assistance Advisory Group, commanded by Lt. Gen. Lionel C. McGarr, and to direct all U.S. troops and other personnel on advisory, training and support missions with South Vietnamese forces. A Pentagon spokesman said Feb. 9 that the new command was a demonstration of the U.S.' belief that "this is a war we can't afford to lose" and that "we're drawing a line" against Communist subversion in South Vietnam.

The escalation of U.S. involvement in South Vietnam drew a warning from Peking. A Communist Chinese Foreign Ministry statement broadcast Feb. 24, 1962 by Peking radio said that the U.S. intervention was "a direct threat" to Communist North Vietnam and hence "seriously affects the security of China and the peace of Asia." The statement charged that the new U.S. command in South Vietnam was "by no means merely one for military assistance but an operational command of the United States imperialists for direct participation.... The United States is already in an 'undeclared war' in South Vietnam." Communist China called on Britain and the USSR, co-chairmen of the 1954 Geneva conference on Indochina, to take "apropriate measures" to deal with the U.S. actions.

Soviet Deputy Foreign Min. Valerian A. Zorin said at a UN press conference Feb. 26 that the U.S. risked becoming "bogged down in a very disadvantageous and politically unjustified war" in South Vietnam. He warned that the U.S.' continued involvement could "entail very unpleasant consequences."

Tension in Taiwan Straits

In June 1962, Communist China massed troops and jet planes in Fukien Province opposite the Chinese Nationalist-held islands of Quemoy and Matsu. Communist China June 23 admitted its military preparations and called for a nationwide alert against what it said would be a U.S.-sponsored invasion of the Chinese mainland from Taiwan.

A Peking warning against possible U.S. military intervention was delivered to the new U.S. ambassador to Poland, John Moors Cabot, by Chinese Amb. Wang Ping-nan in Warsaw June 23. Cabot assured Wang that the U.S. would not support a Nationalist invasion of China. But he expressed U.S. concern over the Communist mobilization and emphasized that the U.S. was treaty-bound to defend the Nationalists against any attack on Taiwan or the Pescadores Islands, off the west coast of Taiwan.

The U.S. and Communist China had maintained channels of communication in Warsaw and at the Geneva conference on Laos as the U.S. involvement in South Vietnam deepened. Peking had sought still another avenue: Communist Chinese Foreign Min. Chen Yi, in an interview with Reuters' general manager Walton A. Cole Oct. 11, 1961, had proposed talks between Communist China and the U.S. on the foreign ministerial level. Chen, interviewed in Peking, had said that such talks could help both sides prepare for an eventual summit meeting between the 2 countries that might ease mutual tensions. The U.S. would have to initiate the meetings because "we have done all we can," Chen declared. He pointed out that U.S.-Communist Chinese meetings were already in progress on the ambassadorial level in Warsaw and on the deputy foreign ministerial level in Geneva.

Pres. Kennedy and U.S. State Secy. Rusk Oct. 11 had rejected Chen Yi's proposal on the ground that Washington and Peking did not have formal diplomatic relations with each other. The Warsaw ambassadorial talks were recessed Nov. 28 until Feb. 6, 1962. The announcement of the recess was made in Warsaw by Communist Chinese Amb. Wang Ping-nan and the outgoing U.S. Amb.-to-Poland Jacob D. Beam. Beam's place as ambassador was taken thereafter by John Moors Cabot.

Chen Cheng, Nationalist Chinese vice president and premier, acknowledged the massing of Communist forces in Fukien Province in a speech June 23, 1962 before a closed meeting in Taipei of the Planning Commission for the Recovery of the Mainland. Chen reported on what he described as "the brightening prospects of fighting back to the lost mainland."

Chinese Communist Foreign Min. Chen Yi declared June 25 that China was "watching vigilantly" what he charged were U.S.-Nationalist preparations for "a large-scale military adventure involving the invasion of the coastal areas of the mainland." The Canton (Fukien) radio reported June 25 that the city's workers had been placed in a state of "voluntary mobilization" to await government orders "to go into action."

Pres. Kennedy declared June 27 that the U.S. "would not remain inactive" if a Chinese Communist assault against Quemoy and Matsu appeared to threaten Taiwan. In an opening statement at his news conference, Kennedy said: The U.S. position must "be clearly understood" in view of the fact that the Chinese military moves in the Taiwan area were "not clear"; the Administration supported policies of ex-Pres. Eisenhower that had called for Communist China's agreement "to the mutual renunciation of the use of force" in the Taiwan area; in the event of "agressive action against" Quemoy and Matsu, the U.S. would "take the action necessary to assure the defense of Formosa and the Pescadores" as provided for in the "Formosa Resolution" adopted by Congress in 1955; "any threat to the offshore islands must be judged in relation to its wider meaning for the safety of Formosa and the peace of the area"; "exactly what action would be necessary in the event of" aggression "would depend on the situation as it developed"; the U.S. purposes in the Taiwan area were "peaceful and defensive."

Nationalist Chinese military officials in Taipei estimated June 29 that the Communists had massed 600,000 troops opposite Quemoy and Matsu, 200,000 more than the previous week. The Nationalists had increased their air and naval patrols around the offshore islands and had alerted their forces in the Pescadores off Taiwan.

Chinese Communist Foreign Min. Chen Yi blamed the U.S. July 1 for creating "tension" in the Taiwan Straits. He said the U.S. would be held responsible "for any action taken by the Chiang Kai-shek gang."

Soviet Premier Khrushchev pledged July 2 that the

USSR would aid Communist China in repelling an assault on the mainland that he said was being prepared by Chiang with "the support of the aggressive circles" of the U.S. In a nationwide TV report on a tour he had made of Rumania, Khrushchev asserted: "Anyone who dares attack" China "will meet a crushing rebuff from the great Chinese people, the peoples of the Soviet Union and the whole Socialist camp"; the dispatch of U.S. 7th Fleet ships to Taiwan showed that the U.S. had an "interest in kindling a new hotbed of war, in increasing international tensions in the Far East"; "this is not the first time that imperialists are trying to test the power of. . . Soviet-Chinese friendship."

U.S. State Secy. Dean Rusk July 2 dismissed as "nonsense" Khrushchev's charges that U.S. "aggressive" circles were supporting a possible Nationalist attack against the mainland. Rusk said the U.S. had called for the "abandonment of force in settling matters in the Formosan Strait."

Sino-Indian Border War

While Peking made no overt attempt to invade the Nationalist-held islands in the Taiwan Straits, Communist Chinese troops staged massive attacks in Oct.-Nov. 1962 in another territorial dispute, that with India.

Throughout 1961 and 1962, the Indian government had strengthened India's border defenses along the Himalayas, and small-scale armed clashes had increased in number. Indian Prime Min. Jawaharlal Nehru stated Oct. 12, 1962 that he had ordered the Indian command to drive all Chinese out of Indian territory in the North East Frontier Agency. The Peking government seized the occasion to unleash massive attacks all along the McMahon Line. The attacks commenced Oct. 20. Chinese Communist troops occupied all of the disputed territory in Kashmir. On the eastern front, the Chinese troops Nov. 19 captured Bomdi La in the western sector of the North East Frontier Agency. The fall of the village and an accompanying flanking movement that cut off the Indian garrisons at nearby Se La and Dirang Dzong placed Chinese troops 25 air miles and 80 road miles from India's Assam State. Civilians had already been evacuated from Bomdi La and Dirang Dzong.

India was reported Oct. 17 to have appealed to the U.S. for military aid. High-altitude transport planes was one item that India was said to have particularly requested. The U.S. State Department, professedly shocked by the Chinese incursion, let it be known Oct. 21 that it would consider sympathetically India's request.

Communist Chinese Premier Chou En-lai warned Nov. 13 that U.S. military aid to India would cause the border war to spread to the disadvantage of Afro-Asian nations as well as to India and China. Chou asserted that the U.S. was "overtly sending military aid to India" and planned to "station a big supply mission" there. Chou appealed to Afro-Asian governments to condemn any "foreign intervention" in the Chinese-Indian conflict.

Indian Prime Min. Nehru soon turned largely to the U.S. for military assistance, principally because the Soviet Union was prevented from aiding India by Moscow's treaty of friendship, cooperation and mutual assistance with Peking. Nehru told his parliament Nov. 14 that the USSR's "good wishes" for India "are a great consolation to us, and we hope we will have them in the future." Repeating the view that the USSR was in a difficult position because of its alliance with China and its friendship for India, Nehru said: "We must realize we cannot suggest they go against allies." Nehru made the statement after having conferred earlier Nov. 14 with Soviet Amb.-to-India Ivan Benediktov.

A formal request for "massive" U.S. military aid was made by Nehru in a letter delivered Nov. 19 to Pres. Kennedy by Indian Amb.-to-U.S. Braj Kumar Nehru. The letter reportedly did not request specific weapons but gave details of the fighting and cited India's desperate defense needs.

(The U.S. already had filled 3 of the 5 weapons-request lists submitted by India in the past 3 weeks. The other requests, for artillery, road-building equipment and transport planes, had been partly filled.) The Kennedy-Amb. Nehru conference was attended by State Secy. Dean Rusk and several of his aides, including Assistant State Secy. (for Near Eastern & Southeast Asian affairs) Philips Talbot.

Kennedy announced at his news conference Nov. 20 that a U.S. mission, headed by Assistant State Secy. (for Far Eastern affairs) W. Averell Harriman and Assistant Defense Secy. Paul H. Nitze would fly to New Delhi Nov. 21 to determine what additional U.S. arms India needed to help repel Chinese attacks. (The mission was prompted by complaints from U.S. officials that they knew too little of the Indian army's capabilities and requirements.) Other members of the U.S. mission included Roger Hilsman, State Department director of intelligence and research; Carl Kaysen, a White House aide; Deputy Assistant State Secy. (for South Asian affairs) James P. Grant; and Gen. Paul D. Adams, commander of the U.S.' Strike Command. Kennedy, attempting to quiet Pakistani objections to U.S. military aid to India, said: "Chinese incursions into the subcontinent are a threat to Pakistan as well as India, and both have a common interest in opposing it"; U.S. aid to India "in no way diminishes or qualifies our commitment to Pakistan."

British Prime Min. Harold Macmillan announced in the House of Commons Nov. 20 that Britain was considering increasing its military aid to India. 3 Royal Air Force planes left Singapore for India Nov. 20 with urgently-requested arms. Britain agreed to send India 150 tons of arms in 12 air transport flights in 4 or 5 days.

Communist China announced Nov. 21, 1962 that it was ordering its troops to halt fighting along the entire India-China battle front. The cease-fire was ordered effective at midnight. Peking, in a 2,000-word statement, also said that starting Dec. 1, "Chinese frontier guards will withdraw to positions 20 kilometers [12.43 miles] behind the lines of actual control which existed between China and India" Nov. 7, 1959. This pullback, according to Peking, would move Chinese troops to the north of the McMahon Line in the northeast and to the north of their current positions in Ladakah in the west. The statement said the Chinese action was aimed at ending hostilities and at putting into effect Peking's Oct. 24 border proposals (calling for Indian and Chinese forces to withdraw 20 kilometers pending "peaceful negotiations"), which had been rejected by India.

Chinese Communist Premier Chou En-lai had indicated Peking's preference for such a course of action in replies sent Nov. 13 to mediation proposals by Guinea, Tanganyika and the United Arab Republic (from Pres. Gamal Abdel Nasser) and published in Peking newspapers Nov. 19. Chou rejected the Tanganyikan and UAR proposals but praised the proposal of Guinean Pres. Sékou Touré as "equitable, constructive and conducive to a peaceful settlement" of the conflict. Touré's proposal, submitted Nov. 6, had called for: (a) an immediate cease-fire; (b) mutual troop withdrawals to 20 kilometers from the "natural boundary"; (c) an immediate Chinese-Indian meeting "with a view to settling their dispute by peaceful negotiation"; (d) "outright condemnation" by India and China "of all foreign intervention" in the conflict.

Chou, in letters sent to 24 African and Asian governments and made public Nov. 17, had appealed for their influence to "facilitate the peaceful settlement of the Indian-Chinese boundary question on a fair and reasonable basis." Chou said in his letter: India had tried to "obstruct the peaceful [Communist Chinese] liberation of Tibet in 1950"; India had "laid claim to large tracts of Chinese territory" in 1959 "after the rebellion in Tibet"; the India-China border conflict "was wholly engineered by the Indian government deliberately and over a long period of time."

Peking acted unilaterally in ending the fighting. Peking

said that it "reserved the right to fight back in self-defense" in the event of any of these 3 "possibilities": (1) If Indian troops "continued their attacks after the Chinese frontier guards had ceased fire and when they are withdrawing"; (2) if "the Indian troops [after the Chinese withdrawal] should again advance to the line of actual control in the eastern sector, *i.e.*, the illegal McMahon Line, and/or... refuse to withdraw but remain on the line of actual control in the middle of the western sectors"; (3) if after the Chinese withdrawal, Indian troops "cross the line of actual control and recover their positions prior to Sept. 8."

The Chinese statement also said: Bilateral discussion of the Chinese troop withdrawal could start "immediately" "provided that the Indian government agreed to corresponding measures"; the 2-country talks could take up the establishment of checkposts by both sides and the return of prisoners; following the implementation of those agreements, Prime Min. Nehru and Chinese Premier Chou En-lai could meet to discuss an over-all border settlement; China would establish checkposts to insure normal movement for border-area residents and to "forestall the activities of saboteurs and maintain order"; in the past 2 years Indian troops had crossed "the line of actual control between China and India and nibbled Chinese territory, set up strongpoints for aggression and provoked a number of border clashes"; Nehru's Nov. 1 border proposals were "unreasonable" because they required China to "cede 5,000 to 6,000 more square miles of Chinese territory"; China hoped that India would "make a positive response" to Peking's latest proposals; if New Delhi "fails to make such a response," China would take the initiative.

An Indian government spokesman complained unofficially that the Nov. 21 midnight cease-fire order gave the Chinese "time to occupy still more of our territory before they halt their aggression." He said: If the proposed Chinese troop withdrawal were conditioned "on a corresponding withdrawal by us, then tonight's [Chinese] declaration is only a ruse"; an Indian pullback "means we would have to withdraw from positions we occupy even now in the face of their [Chinese] aggression"; India did not believe that the Chinese were offering a unilateral withdrawal to permit Indian forces to reoccupy territory already taken by the Chinese; the Chinese "seem to be seeking in their reference to. . .[Peking's] unacceptable [border] proposal of last Oct. 24. . .recognition by India of their move into Ladakh."

Nehru Dec. 12 supported the Communist Chinese peace proposals with reservations. Speaking to parliament, Nehru said that India did not "wish to impede" implementation of the truce plan but that it could give "no guarantee" to observe it in the future. Nehru explained: "That depends on circumstances. For the present we are accepting the cease-fire, but it all depends on what the Chinese may or may not do in the future." Nehru listed Indian casualties in the border fighting since Oct. 20 at 197 killed, 291 wounded and 5,174 still unaccounted for. Nehru said the Chinese had claimed holding 1,102 Indian prisoners.

Soviet Premier Khrushchev, in a Moscow speech Dec. 12, lauded the Chinese proposals and called Western military aid to India "a noose around her neck."

Indian officials reentered Bomdi La Dec. 16 and assumed control of the civilian administrative headquarters of the Kameng division of the North East Frontier Agency. Chinese troops had withdrawn from Bomdi La Dec. 13 as part of a general troop pullback which reportedly had started Dec. 1 in accordance with Peking's proposals. Indian civilian scouts also had confirmed the withdrawal of Chinese soldiers up to Michuka in the Siano division and Walong in the Lohit division of the northeast.

The *Christian Science Monitor* reported Dec. 19 that Nehru, in a letter to North Vietnamese Pres. Ho Chi Minh, had called China's invasion of India a calculated and premeditated act that must be undone before India could negotiate or accept China's cease-fire proposals. Nehru's letter was in response to a note from Ho urging India to accept Peking's proposals.

Eventually, however, both India and China accepted in principle the 6-nation Colombo plan for ending the Indian-Chinese border dispute.

Indian agreement was announced by Nehru in parliament Jan. 23, 1963. Nehru, whose announcement was greeted with shouts of "appeasement" by some parliament members, said the proposals "in essence meet our demand that the *status quo* before Sept. 8 [1962] be restored before talks with China can take place." Nehru said that Ceylonese Prime Min. Sirimavo Bandaranaike, who had presented the Colombo plan to him and Chinese Premier Chou En-lai, had informed him that Chou had "accepted the proposals in principle but maintains his own interpretation of these." Chou, according to Mrs. Bandaranaike, had asked for direct talks with Nehru to settle their apparent different interpretations of the Colombo plan. Nehru, referring to this request, said: "Obviously China does not accept wholly the Colombo proposals"; "there cannot be preliminary talks unless China accepts fully."

Chou had accepted the plan at meetings with Mrs. Bandaranaike in Peking Jan. 1–4. A Chinese communiqué Jan. 7 said the Peking government had given "a positive response" to the proposals. The communiqué said that "in the interest of Asian-African solidarity it is imperative that a solution to the Sino-Indian boundary question be found without delay. . . ."

The Sino-Indian border plan had been drawn up in Colombo, Ceylon Dec. 10–12, 1962 at a meeting of 6 non-aligned nations (Ceylon, Burma, the UAR, Cambodia, Ghana and Indonesia). Major points of the plan, made public Jan. 19: (a) ". . . The existing *de facto* cease-fire is a good starting point for a peaceful settlement" of the dispute. (b) In the western sector (Ladakh area of Kashmir), Chinese troops should "carry out their" plan to withdraw 12 miles from the current positions as proposed by Chou to Nehru Nov. 21 and 28, 1962. Indian troops should "keep their existing military position." (c) "Pending a final solution of the border dispute, the area vacated by the Chinese military will be a demilitarized zone to be administered by civilian posts of both sides. . .without prejudice to the rights of the previous presence of both India and China in that area." (d) In the eastern sector (the North East Frontier Agency), "the line of actual control in the areas recognized by both" India and China "could serve as a cease-fire line to their respective positions. Remaining areas in this sector can be settled in their future discussions." (e) Indian-Chinese border disputes in "the middle sector" should "be solved by peaceful means. . ." (f) These proposals, "which could help in consolidating the cease-fire, once implemented, should pave the way for [bi-lateral] discussion[s]. . .for the purpose of solving problems entailed in the cease-fire position." (g) ". . . Positive response for the proposed appeal will not prejudice" the Chinese or Indian "position. . .as regards its conception of the final alignment of the boundaries."

Sino-Soviet Dispute

After the Sino-Indian border war, the ideological dispute between Moscow and Peking became more intense and vitriolic; at the same time, Communist China's antagonism toward the U.S. increased. Washington sought to keep aloof from but closely abreast of the Sino-Soviet rift.

Pres. Kennedy in an interview with a Japanese trade delegation Dec. 3, 1962, expressed his concern with Communist China. He said: "Our problem now, of course, is that with the rise of the Communist power in China combined with an expansionistic Stalinist philosophy, our major problem. . .is how we can contain the expansion of communism in Asia so that we do not find the Chinese moving out into a dominant position in all of Asia.... There are a billion people in the Communist empire operating from central lines and in a belligerent phase of their national development."

In a televised interview Dec. 17, Kennedy stressed the importance of preventing the Communist movement from being dominated by Communist China. "We would be far worse off—the world would be—if the Chinese dominated the Communist movement, because they believe in war as a means of bringing about the Communist world," he declared.

The U.S., Britain and the Soviet Union initialed a partial nuclear weapons test-ban treaty July 25, 1963 in Moscow. *Peking Review* Aug. 9 called it a "tripartite treaty...aimed at tying China's hands." There followed a series of vituperative charges exchanged between Moscow and Peking.

A Communist Chinese government statement broadcast Aug. 15 by Peking radio charged that the USSR had offered in 1957 to help Communist China produce nuclear bombs but had withdrawn its offer in 1959 to placate the U.S. The Chinese statement was in reply to a Soviet statement published Aug. 3 denouncing a July 31 Peking attack on the treaty. The Chinese statement of Aug. 15 said, in part: "It is no new story that Soviet leaders, in collusion with American imperialism, plot to bind China hand and foot." "On June 20, 1959, when there was no hint of the so-called nuclear test-ban treaty, the Soviet government unilaterally scrapped the Oct. 15, 1957 agreement concerning new defense technology [and] refused to supply China with atomic bomb samples and technical materials for the manufacture of atomic bombs, apparently as a gift for...[Khrushchev] to take to Eisenhower when visiting the United States in September."

The USSR replied with a lengthy statement issued Aug. 21 through the Tass news agency. The Russian statement defended the nuclear test-ban treaty and charged that Communist China's opposition to the pact proved that its leaders did not care "how nuclear arms spread among the capitalist states as long as the Chinese leaders got a chance to lay their hands on a nuclear bomb and see what it is like." The Soviet statement charged that "some people in Peking are ready to sacrifice half the population of their country, half of entire mankind," in a nuclear war. It added that mainland China was not able to produce nuclear weapons in quantity and that even if it were able to make "2 or 3 bombs" it still would be dependent on the USSR's "nuclear shield" for protection. It implied that Communist China had harmed this shield when it made public in its statement "classified . . . information related to the defense of the countries of the Socialist community."

(The Soviet government statement was issued in the midst of a virulent Soviet press campaign against Communist China. The Communist Party newspaper *Pravda* charged Aug. 16 that Communist China had "taken advantage" of the 1962 crisis over the Cuban missile bases to launch its military campaign against India. The unofficial Soviet government newspaper *Izvestia* asserted Aug. 23 that Communist China had broken the "laws of international relations" in a way reminiscent of "the most outrageous aggressors and villains, such as Attila, . . . Genghis Khan, . . . Napoleon and Hitler." *Izvestia*, rejecting Chinese charges that Russian food prices were high, said Aug. 24 that "strict food rationing has existed there [in mainland China] since 1954, and in recent years there has been rationing for practically all consumer goods.")

The Chinese Communist Party responded with a 10,000-word statement issued in Peking Sept. 1. The Chinese statement, rejecting the USSR's "gross and fantastic lies" about Peking's policy, said, "apparently the Soviet leaders have already become so degenerate that they now depend on telling lies for a living." The statement denied that Communist China had been the one to reveal Soviet-bloc defense secrets. Addressing itself to Soviet leaders, it said: "Please do not pretend innocence. You know very well that long before we published our last statement you told the Americans secrets between China and the Soviet Union concerning nuclear weapons." "The Soviet leaders are perhaps too hasty in deriding China for its backwardness. . .[But] even if we Chinese people are unable to produce an atom bomb for 100 years, we will neither crawl to the baton of the Soviet leaders nor kneel before the nuclear blackmail of the U.S. imperialists." Describing the Soviet leaders as "worshippers of nuclear weapons," the Chinese statement also said: "In the opinion of Soviet leaders, in this nuclear century to remain alive is everything and there is no aim in life. This is the philosophy of willing slaves, which demands that they submit to the tender mercies of imperialism. . . . It is a truly bestial concept."

Soviet Premier Khrushchev toured Yugoslavia Aug. 22–Sept. 3. He said in a speech at the Rakovica Automobile Works near Belgrade Aug. 21: "As the Chinese say—they say one thing and do another—they say their country has to rely on its own resources to build socialism. . . . They say they are going to rely on their own resources and then they write us for credits. That is their motto: Our resources and your credits."

Pres. Kennedy at his press conference Aug. 1 had also commented critically on Communist China. Kennedy said that China would threaten the U.S. if Peking continued to adhere to its currently bellicose policies into the decade of the 1970s. He noted that China's limited position as a world power might be substantially changed by the next decade. He said that if China continued its rapid increase toward a population of 700 millions, acquired nuclear weapons and maintained its Stalinist government and policy, it could create a "more dangerous situation than any we faced since the end of the 2d war." Kennedy also said that in comparison with the Chinese, Russian leaders "pursued in most cases their ambitions with some caution."

Chinese Communist Premier Chou En-lai covered a wide range of subjects in an interview given in Peking Oct. 11 to Reuters general manager Gerald Long. Among the principal points of the Chou interview, made public Oct. 13, were these comments on Sino-American relations: Any improvement of U.S.-Chinese relations would be difficult as long as the U.S. maintained its "basic policy" "of aggression and war threats against China." The U.S. was "occupying our territory Taiwan and...carrying out armed threats in the Taiwan Strait." The U.S. "must withdraw" from South Vietnam because "everything that is now taking place" there "has been created by U.S. armed aggression and intervention."

The Chinese Communist Party continued its publication of statements in *Jenmin Jih Pao* (*People's Daily*) and the party theoretical journal *Hung Chi* (*Red Flag*) attacking the Soviet viewpoint:

The 4th statement, issued Oct. 21, accused Soviet leaders of taking a "passive," "scornful" and "negative" attitude toward the Communist movements of Asia, Africa and Latin America. It said: "A great revolutionary storm" had spread through these regions in recent years; this new movement had been fully supported by China but had been covertly stifled by the USSR, whose leaders were "sorely afraid of the...storm"; Soviet leaders had "betrayed the Communist stand of supporting just wars and have sided with imperialism"; they had sought to "subordinate national liberation revolution to their general line of peaceful coexistence and to national interest of their own country."

The 5th attack, published Nov. 18, denounced Khrushchev for advancing the "erroneous military strategy" that nuclear weapons could not be used to insure victory in "a war of national liberation or revolutionary civil war." The statement said: "When Soviet leaders brandish their nuclear weapons, it is not really to support the people's anti-imperialist struggles"; "at...times, during the Caribbean crisis, for instance, they engage in speculative, opportunistic

and irresponsible nuclear gambling for ulterior motives";
Khrushchev's military policy was "based on nuclear fetish-
ism and nuclear blackmail."

The 6th in the series, published Dec. 11, denounced as
an "unprecedented shame" the USSR's "foul practice of
collaboration with the United States imperialists." It said:
"The heart and soul of the general line of peaceful coexistence
pursued by the leaders of the Soviet Communist Party is
Soviet-United States collaboration for domination of the
world"; the USSR was trying to "wreck the Socialist camp"
and impose "class capitulation" instead of carrying out
Leninist policies of unremitting class struggle; "Khrushchev
is impervious to...facts; he...regards the anti-imperialist
struggles of Socialist countries...as incompatible with a
policy of peaceful coexistence."

But rejecting the possibility of a break in Sino-Soviet
relations, Communist Chinese Premier Chou En-lai had said
Oct. 9 that the Peking-Moscow "treaty of alliance and amity
is still alive." Chou made the statement in an interview in
Peking with visiting ex-Japanese Premier Tanzan Ishibashi.
Chou said that Communist China did not want to bring up
the Sino-Soviet ideological controversy "as a political dispute," "but the Soviet Union has brought it up as an international problem." Chou, recalling that "the Soviet Union
had recalled its technical experts from China" in 1962, said
that "China has not asked her technicians in the Soviet Union
to return home. Neither will China recall her students."
Despite Sino-Soviet differences, "China will not go to such
extremes as breaking diplomatic relations or start a war,"
Chou asserted. Chou said: "If East Germany is invaded,
Communist China will go to its aid. If China should be
invaded, we have faith the Soviet Union will come to our
aid."

The Soviet Communist Party appealed to Communist
parties throughout the world Oct. 23 to oppose Communist
Chinese efforts to replace "Leninism with Maoism." The

Soviet party claimed that 65 national Communist parties (out of an estimated 86) supported Moscow in its ideological dispute with China. The Soviet plea, made in the theoretical journal *Kommunist*, warned that if Chinese efforts to dominate the world Communist scene were not stopped, "the consequences for the entire Communist movement may be very grave." *Kommunist* charged that: (a) China was supporting "anti-party groups" in other countries in an effort to form them into a new "international bloc" made up largely "of people who have been expelled from Communist parties"; (b) China had revived the Stalinist "personality cult" because it needed Stalin's name.

UN Bars Peking

Amid the intensifying exchange of polemics between the 2 Communist giants, the UN General Assembly Oct. 21, 1963 rejected by 57–41 vote (with 12 abstentions and Ethiopia absent) an Albanian proposal to expel the Nationalist Chinese delegation and seat in its place the representatives of Communist China. The margin of defeat was slightly larger than it had been in 1962, when the vote was 56–42. A $\frac{2}{3}$ majority, 74 affirmative votes, would have been required for adoption of the proposal. U.S. Amb.-to-UN Adlai E. Stevenson said Oct. 21 that the vote was evidence of the Assembly's "strong" aversion to seating the Peking régime.

The draft resolution on China had been introduced in the Assembly Oct. 16 by Albanian Foreign Min. Behar Shtylla; it had been presented in past years by the Soviet Union. The change in the draft's sponsorship reflected the ideological and political estrangement between the USSR and Red China. Shtylla declared that Peking's exclusion was "unjust and absurd" in view of being organized by the U.S., the sole source of real support for "the Chiang Kai-shek phantom" régime on Taiwan. Nationalist Chinese delegate Liu Chieh replied that his government was the only legitimate representative of the Chinese people. Soviet Amb.-to-UN Nikolai T. Fedorenko addressed the Assembly in support of the draft Oct. 21 but did not refer to Shtylla's speech nor praise the Peking régime.

Kennedy Slain; Chou's Reaction

U.S. Pres. John F. Kennedy was assassinated in Dallas, Tex. Nov. 22, 1963.

Asked during his visit to the United Arab Republic to comment on Kennedy's assassination, Communist Chinese Premier Chou En-lai said in Cairo Dec. 2 that it was a "despicable, shameful act." The Communists opposed any kind of assassination "even if the one assassinated is hostile to China," Chou said.

179